ARAFAT'S HAND

For my parents

ARAFAT'S HAND
A Sojourn in the Occupied West Bank

Roy Sturgess

William Sessions Limited
York, England

© Roy Sturgess 2000

ISBN 1 85072 255 2

Printed in 11 on 12 point Plantin Typeface
from Author's Disk
by Sessions of York
The Ebor Press
York YO31 9HS, England

Contents

Chapter		Page
	Acknowledgements	vi
	Author's note	vi
	Introduction	viii
1	Newcastle to Nablus, summer-autumn 1995	1
2	Holding Our Lives Together: Palestinian Refugees, 1947-95	8
3	Nablus, October 1995	25
4	Khalil	52
5	On the Road to Jerusalem	58
6	Refugees at Home: Balata camp	66
7	Walid	81
8	Ruth and Afif	86
9	Ibrahim and Mona	89
10	Newcastle	97
11	Nablus, September 1997	99
12	Newcastle	108
	Bibliography	109
	Index	111

List of Illustrations

Israel, the West Bank and Gaza Strip	x
Fari'a camp	11
Nablus Old City	27
Nablus. Old City wall	28
Nablus. Dancing in the streets after the Israeli withdrawal	42
Batala camp alleyway; sewage channel on left	67
Gaza city. Street scene after January rain	91
Rooftops in Gaza city	91

Acknowledgements

I OWE MY GREATEST debt to Najeh Jarrar. Without his initiative and companionship the writing of this book would never have been possible. These pages are meant as some little recompense for the joint book that never came to be. My thanks also to An Najah University for having me stay there from October 1995 to January 1996. I am grateful to Gordon Smith for listening creatively at the very beginning. For cajoling, criticising and sustaining me on the way I particularly want to thank Julia Gordon, Trevor Leonard, Sue and George Henderson-Smyth, Mark Burns and my daughter Judy Sturgess. Walter Storey offered revealing insights. My thanks to Dr Ibrahim Al-Fanni and Nablus Municipality for making available a map of the town. It will become clear to the reader how great a debt of gratitude I owe to unnamed individuals in the text.

Author's Note

BECAUSE IT IS NOT always safe to air opinions publicly in the areas where I stayed or travelled, all the people mentioned in the text, unless they have a high public profile, are given pseudonyms.

We gathered in a large square on the edge of town. A gaol for political prisoners, only just abandoned by Israeli soldiers, took up one side of the square. After nearly an hour two helicopters circled and descended into the grounds of the gaol, while another helicopter of a different design continued hovering high above. 'These are Arafat's helicopters, they are lent by Egypt for ceremonial occasions,' my friend said. 'The other is Israeli. They never let him out of their sight'. Soon Arafat's voice echoed through the public address system. 'There he is,' said someone, pointing to the roof of the gaol, 'that's his hand.' Everyone round me stared into the glare of the sun that came directly from above the gaol. We had waited an hour for this moment. Yet, high above us, surrounded by his soldiers and in front of many thousands of his own people, Arafat hid behind his lieutenants, revealing only a waving hand to the crowd.

Introduction

IT IS DECEMBER 1999 and I am sitting surrounded by notes, seeking meaning in my visits to the West Bank in 1995-96 and 1997. How can I deal with those months? The darkening events, the constant up-rush of feelings, the complex interaction of emotion and politics, the small triumphs and lasting tragedies in friends' lives, the watching as people try to make sense of it all; and all the time aware of being neither fully an observer nor fully a participant. Finally, a question: can writing be a work of healing and reconciliation as well as an attempt at explanation?

An early memory is of Pathe News pictures of the gates of Belsen Camp being opened. My recollection is one of incomprehension, I think the most I could do was to see this as a sombre reminder of what could happen in places far away, a bestial development made possible only on some unclear borderland of war. Over a decade later, I realised that the Christian culture I grew up in included a clear if painful space for the dilemmas of assimilated Jews. Jewish friends occasionally mentioned memories of their parents' escape from 1930s Germany and the psychological price they were still paying for this. More rarely, a reference would be made to the mark left on collective memory by earlier Christian persecution of Jews or by the Churches' failure to speak up for them in times of crisis. In a sense I'd picked up these feelings already. The introspective manner of my two friends seemed to say more about the weight of history than did the occasionally awkward religious/historical lacunae in conversations.

Yet it took a tremendous leap of imagination to reconcile the diffidence of my friends with the confident words and demeanour of Israeli political and military leaders represented by newsreels of the same period. Just as puzzling were the almost exclusive television images I remember of Israel: members of war cabinets in urgent conclave and Israeli tanks and planes traversing expanses of desert in displays of military skill and daring. For, now, the enemy was the Arabs.

The cultural space given to Arabs during my youth was small by comparison. I remember only a resounding ignorance that society and my schooling did little to remove. An exception was Lawrence of Arabia. These stories catered for a sense of adventure and therefore made no attempt to explain the complexities of Arab life. They also centred on Lawrence himself – the Arabs were colourful background – and they defined Arabs as a contingent people, galvanised into meaningful action only by western military needs.

Even now explanations for my desire to go to the West Bank do not come smoothly to mind. I don't remember that I had ONE big reason. However it started and however much I thought myself in control of events, the impetus to go grew until it took me over. Recent divorce, feelings of being only a visitor in a new flat, drifting from café to café in the time made available by retirement, everything tasted of emptiness and failure. I didn't want to stay like this but couldn't find the strength or purpose to do any other. For some while though I'd felt a growing desire to live in a totally different culture from the ones I knew, somewhere with its own strong identity, as little affected by Europe and America as I could find. A friend's anecdotes of years spent in the Middle East had touched a deep spot. I imagined Arab life to offer an appreciation of the unsaid and to contain social relations that acknowledged and nourished a need for human bonding and responsibilities. I did not yet realise that my 'freedom' of the last few years had in fact become a thinly disguised chaos as I shed familiar connections at a furious rate. I also wanted to link up with people with whom I felt an affinity – refugees. I'd been drawn to working with them locally without bothering to analyse why. The first foreign locus of refugees I thought of was the West Bank. Also, I felt a strong need to do something with my academic skills that related to people's issues in the here-and-now. The sterility of my last few working years had left me wanting to feel truly alive. Dismay with what I perceive universities usually offer young people – the narrowing focus on mental exercise – had set in a while before retirement. In other words, without understanding this yearning, I wanted to feel connected and purposeful. Searching for contact with refugees I wrote to two Palestinian universities. One replied within a few weeks.

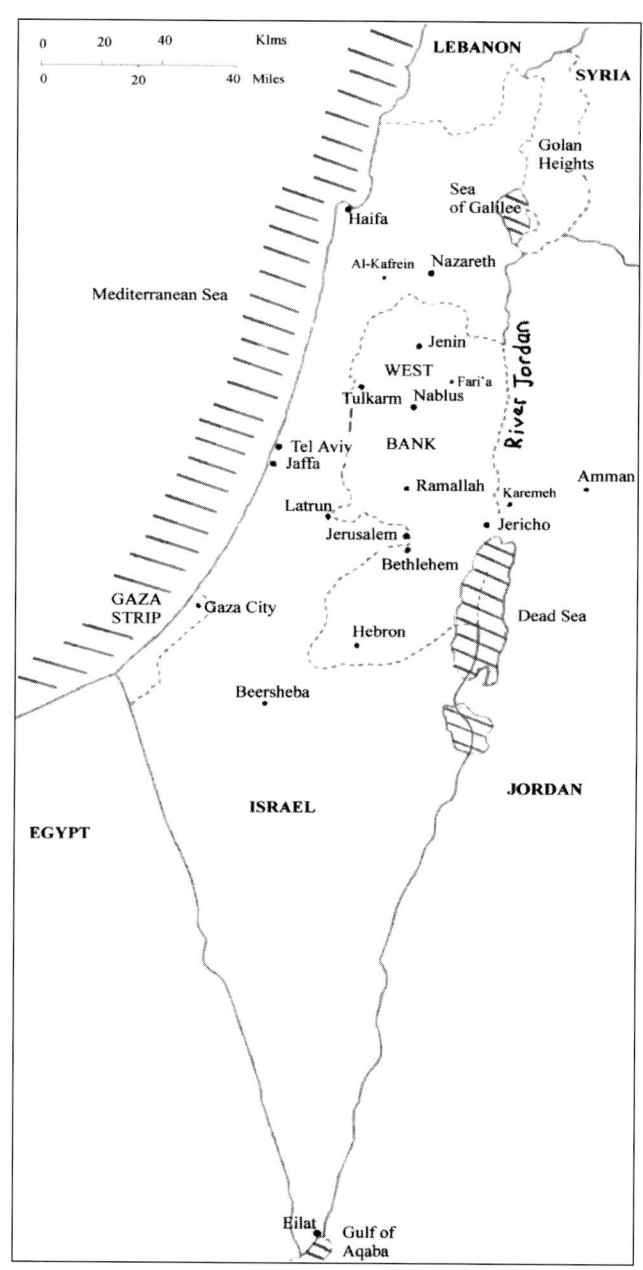

Israel, the West Bank and Gaza Strip.

CHAPTER 1

Newcastle to Nablus, summer-autumn 1995

THE ENVELOPE HAS an eagle crest and an Israeli stamp. 'The Palestinians face a tremendous phenomenon: the refugee problem,' writes my unknown correspondent. 'Three camps of these refugees surround the City of Nablus where our University is located.' Come and stay for three months if you are interested, there may be a joint project here, he went on. Some part of me (the magical part?) has been waiting for this reply for a month, barely believing it might come. Many confused issues are now simplified. Yes! I am interested.

* * *

The regular layout of Tel Aviv lay below as the plane descended towards Israeli soil. Ben Gurion is Israel's international airport and, located near the Mediterranean coast, it is a long way from my present, inland destination. Nablus is in the north of the area known as the West Bank, that is, the west bank of the River Jordan. The state of Jordan is on the east bank of the river. The area to the west of the river has had many names in its long history – Canaan, Judea and Samaria and Palestine among them. As I brace myself to enter an un-seasonally hot October in a few moments I pondered the oddity of attaching the name 'West Bank' to this remnant of the British Mandate of Palestine, a name that has no standing in history or law, despite its geographical literalness. This oddity is at the heart of the dilemma thrown up by the strained political history of the eastern Mediterranean in this century.

* * *

The whole of the eastern Mediterranean coastline from the Bosphorus to the Sinai desert was part of the Turkish Ottoman Empire at the beginning of the last century. The Ottoman Turks went to war in 1914, siding with Germany against an Anglo-French-Russian alliance, because they feared dismemberment by western powers and they wanted the return of territory lost to Russia in the previous century. The large and scattered Ottoman Empire was finding modernisation a slow business, it was saddled with a cumbersome bureaucracy and could easily be seen as a prey by more westernised countries. It did not give its Arab dominions a high priority, even though Ottoman rulers had realised for some time that pan-Islamism was a potent weapon against an intrusive West. By failing to act on this issue it may have passed up its last chance to survive as a great power. An incipient nationalism in Arab towns reflected the growing power of a modernisation movement at the centre of the empire in the dying years of the 19th century. In the meantime Jews imbued with European attitudes began to flee from racial attacks and to settle in this outpost of the Ottoman Empire. They began to build the town of Tel Aviv along European lines in 1909. These developments were watched with a benign eye by the imperial authorities, the Ottomans having traditionally been tolerant hosts to non-Islamic minorities.

The anti-Jewish pogroms that raged through Russia, Roumania and Eastern Europe before the turn of the century convinced a small number of Jews that attempts to assimilate into indigenous peoples had failed. These radical Jews, calling themselves Zionists, wanted a Jewish homeland. Their talks with European governments had yielded a British offer of a settlement in Uganda. This was their best hope until the Great War rearranged western priorities. This new Jewish movement grew up in a world with little knowledge of or care for peoples who had not reached the stage of economic and constitutional development enjoyed by the West, these peoples being thought worthy of redemption but not of equal treatment. Many leaders in the advanced world took it as a nostrum that to implant people with a western outlook into an area of traditional peoples would bring great benefits to the latter. That this might entail the displacement or alienation of the host population was not yet widely viewed with the moral repugnance of the second half of the 20th century. Most of the Jews who settled in the Holy Land in the century before 1920 believed they were the vanguard of a return to their Promised Land. An increasing number thought in terms of statehood. The influx – 65,000 between 1882 and 1914 – although fiercely resented by Arabs, was as yet not large enough to upset the broad demographic balance, except in Jerusalem, where substantial numbers were living by the turn of the century. They bought property from Arab leaders or effendi, many of whom lived in Beirut or other distant towns. The Great War changed all this. By the autumn of 1917 things were going badly for Britain. The slaughter at Passchendaele coincided with the disabling of her French ally. America had only just entered the war. Driven by a diversity of imperatives – the need for financial and moral succour, hope of influencing American public opinion, a desire to get white support on the ground for British imperial aims in the Middle East, a Christian belief that Jews had been badly done by, which was reflected in the cabinet and supported by well-placed Jews – Britain offered the Jews a homeland in Palestine if Germany and her Turkish ally were defeated. The third aliyah (ascent) after the Great War strengthened an earlier trend in Palestine towards Jewish exclusivity. Most immigrants were European Ashkenazi or secular Jews with rural backgrounds who found work on socialist and cooperative Zionist enterprises that aimed at self-sufficiency and therefore did not require Arab labour. After the Great War Palestinian Jewry increasingly adopted European social practices and styles – from trades unions to civil courts, university education, architecture, dress and even mixed bathing – and the Hebrew language. Moreover these settlers had few links with the Eastern and Orthodox (often Arabic-speaking) Jews already established in Jerusalem. Zionism was now becoming manifest as a separate people in communities that were socialist, cooperative and planned and stood apart from Arab villages and urban districts. Few people knew much about the Arabs who occupied this land; perhaps fewer thought their presence would constitute a problem. The British offer to let Jews build a national home in Palestine had indeed stipulated that this should not prejudice the civil and religious rights of the existing non-Jewish population. And at about the same time promises of independence to the Arabs brought them into the war on Britain's side. The incompatibility of these promises came home to roost when Britain assumed the League of Nations' mandate for Palestine at the Peace Conference. She sought the mandate for strategic reasons – to guard her route to the East through the Suez

Canal and to secure access to the new oil wells of Iraq. During the 26 years of the mandate Britain tried to juggle the claims of the two sides, while the Jewish population increased and demanded independence and the Arabs watched as a demographic revolution took place. The Arabs responded partly with talk and exhortation, partly by violence – assault, riot, revolt and guerrilla warfare. As Britain became less able to carry large overseas commitments she was forced to maintain a military presence to keep Arabs and Jews apart.

Then began the campaign of the Nazi and other regimes to exterminate the Jews. Innumerable personal tragedies left their mark on whole communities and later generations. The Holocaust reshaped some of the questions asked of morality and politics in the West. More immediately, some extreme Jewish nationalists displayed a new, harder edge. Armed Jewish groups in Palestine abandoned the reticence of the pre-war years and instigated concerted attacks on the British and Arabs. Pressure grew for Palestine to absorb Jewish survivors. Weary after the Second World War Britain began to shed her colonial possessions. Then the Palestine conflict burst out with renewed vigour after being held in abeyance during the war.

* * *

My journey is to take me eastwards from Ben Gurion airport across the narrow 'waistline' of Israel to Jerusalem, and then northwards to Ramallah in the Israeli-occupied West Bank, before heading further north to Nablus. Exactly where I cross from Israel into the West Bank is a matter of dispute. I will enter the territory as I cross from West to East Jerusalem, the boundary running through the town, according to the Palestinians. This is the so-called Green Line, which delineated the boundary between Israel and the West Bank after the War of 1948. Alternatively, I will cross it after I have passed the city's northern limits and some Israeli settlements, which is the Israeli position. The Israelis have erected a checkpoint between the two peoples well to the north of the city boundary today. I am now in the West Bank. The political significance of this piece of territory is not only to do with its place in religious history, it is also to do with its size. Only 85 miles by 35 at its greatest, it is all the Palestinians have as a homeland outside the Gaza Strip, and the Israelis want to build settlements on it for their increasing number of immigrants.

From the airport to Nablus is only 60 miles, even along the two sides of a triangle my route followed, yet the journey involved four buses and took six hours. I was determined to see as much of the people and places at a human pace as I could, and so I avoided the much quicker taxis. And I was only learning about the exigencies of travelling in an area of military activity as I encountered them. We passed what looked like an arrangement of parts of old military vehicles along the roadside as we neared Jerusalem, presumably from the War of 1948. At first I reacted with discomfort to the eeriness of these ghostly relics. Standing in the open air on perhaps the major highway of Israel where they are clearly meant to catch the eye of Israelis and visitors alike, they set the military past in aspic and give it inordinate importance. I knew that fierce fighting took place along the corridor between Tel Aviv and Jerusalem in 1948 and Jewish victory hung in the balance for a while near Latrun, which we have just passed.

As war- and concentration camp-weary Jews fled Europe after 1945 they found most doors closed. The British tried to limit their number entering Palestine, seeking to balance the plight of the swollen flow of refugees with Arab anger at the sight of parts of Palestine passing out of their hands. Arab violence spread. As fighting escalated in 1947 the British decided to hand the problem of Palestine over to the United Nations. Groups of Jewish extremists immediately harried the British forces. The Jewish defence force was put on a state of war readiness. The United Nations' decision to partition Palestine in November 1947 overjoyed many Jews and stunned the Arabs. Fighting between units of Arabs and Jews raged all over the country. A key engagement that involved regular Jewish and Jordanian units (the latter being part of the British forces in Palestine) took place through the winter and spring of 1948 on a stretch of road that passed Latrun and Kastel and linked the Jewish communities in Tel Aviv and Jerusalem. Armoured cars operated by members of the Palmach, the Jewish mobilised strike force, escorted armoured buses along this road. The wrecks of these vehicles have been left there in tribute to Palmach fighters. When the British left in May 1948 the Jews declared an independent state in the name of Israel. Regular armies from neighbouring Arab countries, mostly ill-equipped and -trained, and badly co-ordinated, then attacked the Israeli forces on behalf of the Arabs of

Palestine. Numerically superior to the Arab forces at the outset, the Jewish army was better trained and rapidly built up its strength. The fighting was fierce and rules of war were stretched. Arabs still lament the villagers massacred in Dir Yassin; Jews remember the Arab retaliation. Of more lasting effect was the displacement of the majority of the Arabs of Palestine, who were forced by Jewish troops or fled in fear of them, especially from areas of mixed Jewish-Arab populations. As Jewish forces moved across the boundaries of the area allotted to them by the United Nations a few months earlier, a mass exodus of Arabs occurred from around Beersheba in the northern Negev; the central zone from West Jerusalem to Jaffa; the coast above and below Haifa; and the Jezreel Valley and Galilee. Something like 750,000 refugees, maybe 75% of the Arab population, fetched up in towns and refugee settlements, or in refugee camps provided by the new United Nations, on the western and southern fringes of old Palestine or beyond its borders. Israel refused to let them return to their homes or to compensate them for their losses. The rump of what was Palestine passed into other hands: Jordan held on to part of eastern Palestine, since called the West Bank, and Egyptian forces retained a small piece of the southern Mediterranean coast (the Gaza Strip). Thousands of Arabs stayed behind Israeli lines and became uneasy citizens, subject to martial law, of a Jewish state. Nineteen years later another war ended with Israel occupying the West Bank and Gaza. All of old Palestine remains under Israeli control in October 1995.

Latrun recedes into the distance and the outskirts of Jerusalem begin to appear. Remembering the military relics that passed a few minutes ago I ponder the concern of the Israeli authorities to fortify a resilient patriotism. Nationhood was achieved almost 50 years ago. The Zionist political mission is virtually complete: Jews now have a democratic state in their historical homeland. Yet, they do not possess the whole of the original homeland. The Land of Israel may have extended across the present West Bank into the modern State of Jordan. This is the irreducible problem – for Israel to try and incorporate the West Bank she risks a scale of internal division that would threaten the very viability of her democracy and maybe, if a resulting war engulfed Israel, the State of Israel itself. Yet she keeps growing. The latest immigrants to arrive left Russia after the collapse of the USSR. However, many of them have only a slight appreciation of Israel's history. And Israel is at war or in a state of preparedness for it on three fronts – Lebanon, Syria and the Palestinians. Moreover, a fourth front can be seen as internal – her own society is deeply split along religious-secular and European-Eastern lines, as well as over the issue of 'land for peace', whether to return land she overran in war for the guarantee of peace. Reasons enough to emphasise the bonds of war and patriotism. About half my fellow bus passengers are soldiers – my first sight of a people's army since my twenties in 1960s Britain. They are mostly in their teens, looking very unmilitary at the moment, as pensive or sleepy as the rest of us. Jerusalem looms ahead – the Eternal City! Yet, after the dramatic hilly scenery a little way back, its western approaches are so drab: a flat expanse of half-completed buildings. There is a delay. The bus driver shouts angrily at a traffic policeman, clearly building up to a confrontation over a road diversion as if it were a personal matter. The policeman shrugs and says something the driver ignores. Although there is some kind of tension in the air, I'm still not fully prepared for the emotion aroused by the existence of a boundary and an army of occupation a mile or two across town, of the true meaning of the awful paradox that providing a home for one nation of refugees has helped to make refugees of another.

CHAPTER 2

Holding Our Lives Together: Palestinian Refugees, 1947-95

BETWEEN NABLUS AND Tubas in the northern West Bank, where the road leaves behind the switchback mountain passes and the land sinks slowly to a valley floor, a refugee camp spreads itself across the slope. It has taken its name from the nearby village of Fari'a. Three thousand years ago Abraham probably travelled this route westwards as he made his way up from the River Jordan to the Canaanite town of Shekhem. Nearly 50 years ago the narrow road must often have been choked with refugees fleeing eastwards from the fighting. The camp lies beside an oasis-like clump of trees that denotes water in this parched land. In fact, the trees surround a spring-fed pond and they bring a splash of green to these Samarian hills. Some of the early refugees of 1948, wearily eyeing the mountains and remembering the coastal fields they had hurriedly left only days or weeks earlier, before fighting forced them onto the roads, felt drawn to this sign of water. They say the spring was the reason the United Nations built a camp here in the first place. They settled nearby where the UN leased a patch of land from local farmers in 1949. About 5,000 people had gathered together by 1960. The stories of the families who came here, though possessing the common threads of hunger, bewilderment and anger, have many individual twists, which would form the warp and weft of the new society these refugees were to help create. Fari'a is one of the smallest, most intimate and most homogeneously peasant of the camps in the West Bank yet its short history reflects the lot of camp dwellers in Palestine, one of constant strain as it grappled with philosophies and practices totally alien to the traditional mind, interspersed with occasional violent episodes when external factors pushed the cohesion of the camp to breaking point.

Before 1948 some 80 lowland rural villages in western Palestine were home to the people who were soon to fetch up at Fari'a. Most families came from only three villages on the Mediterranean plain, Al-Kafrien in the vicinity of Haifa being the largest. The name means 'two villages' in Arabic. There was a mosque and an elementary school for boys; a local sheikh had built the school in the 1880s. About 1,000 people lived in the village on some 2750 acres of land belonging to its clans. Wealth was distributed unevenly between these clans. Two or three owned substantial property, including most of the precious irrigated land, while at the other extreme some clans owned virtually nothing, their people working as share croppers or labourers on the farms of the rich. About 8% of the village was public land, which contained about 10 wells or springs and, if Al-Kafrein were typical of many other villages, this land would have been available for the poorest people to glean the corn harvest and plant small crops of their own. The small area of irrigated soil – less than 50 acres – was devoted to crop husbandry and orchards. The tending of crops, a few hundred cows and numerous poultry provided ample work. Nonetheless, in the absence of local industry, 50 men had to travel for work in nearby Haifa. Most villagers lived in mud or mud and cement huts, up to 10 people sharing one 7x8 metre room, a small kitchen and bathroom. The rich had larger, stone-built houses.

Disaster – called Al-Nakba by the Palestinians – struck Al-Kafrien on 12 April 1948,[1] during the civil war that broke out as the British were preparing to leave the country. At the same time that Jewish forces were fighting near Latrun in central Palestine in order to keep open their supply routes to Jerusalem other units were successfully defending their settlement of Mishmar ha-Emeq in the central northern area between Haifa and Jenin. Al-Kafrein and a number of Arab villages were a short distance from Mishmar. The head of the Jewish Agency, David Ben Gurion, agreed with the

---

(1) Walid Khalili, *All That Remains: The Palestinian Villages Occupied and Depopulated by Israel in 1948* (Washington, Institute for Palestine Studies, 1992) pp 44-45. See also Arthur Koestler, *Promise and Fulfilment: Palestine 1917-1949* (London, MacMillan and Co., 1949) pp 158-159.

Jewish military command to attack and destroy Arab villages near the settlement and then use them to train units in fighting in built-up areas. Al-Kafrein was partly destroyed when occupied and was razed with explosives after these exercises. Arab units nearby had withdrawn earlier. Before the engagement it was clear to the villagers that they must fight alone and they would be at the mercy of superior Jewish forces. Their accounts agree on the inadequate supply of weapons to the village right up to the moment of conflict, the failure of groups of volunteers from other Arab countries to provide significant military support, and the superiority of Zionist military tactics, field intelligence and firepower. The villagers appear to have had little training as a fighting force. Social divisions in Arab society crippled attempts to weld the young men into a fighting unit; men from different clans would not cooperate after an altercation occurred. Panic and despair filled the village when some of its men were killed or injured. The old and very young fled, soon to be followed by the young men, leaving their cattle and large moveables. They thought they would be back in a couple of weeks after the Arab governments had defeated the Zionists.[1]

Today's old men well remember their escape from the war zone. It is only 35 miles from Al-Kafrein to Fari'a as the crow flies, but distance was not the issue in 1948. Roads were congested with families struggling to keep children and goods together, the young people walking and the old sitting on overloaded carts. Some families had become scattered, food and water were scarce, the late spring in these parts is dry and arid, insects were rife and hygiene was negligible. Uncertain where to go, families were often on the verge of panic so that contact with other members of their family or clan who had travelled ahead of them, or news about a refugee facility, was a Godsend. The lives of these rural peasants had previously reached no further than the nearest village or town. Virtually no one had entered these mountains before. The mountain people were Palestinians but they had different customs; the refugees were strangers. The escape routes they followed radiated out from their lowland villages; the patterns of dispersal make little geographical sense otherwise, except for the all-pervading desire to escape east-

---

(1) I am grateful to Najeh Jarrar for letting me refer to material in a draft of his Oxford Brookes University PhD thesis in this and the previous paragraph.

wards away from the Zionist soldiers. Inevitably this took most of them into the mountains. They endured an arid summer and miserably snowy winter. Some began moving further east to Jericho in the Jordan Valley where, they had heard, the Red Cross was giving out tents and material aid. They then returned to the hills again en route for Fari'a, because relatives mentioned the water there. The parents of a present-day camp official made five moves before settling at Fari'a. They stayed only three or four months in one village, five years in another. Everyone talks of the shortages of food and shelter, but the central thread in the camp official's account was his education. He speaks of his family's moves in terms of the school grade he studied in each place. From one village he had to walk six kilometres every day to school across stony mountain slopes. These were 'very bad years'. His measured words seem to reflect his concern to live in the present moment – he also said that every cup of coffee is good now, compared to that time.

These field workers of the western plain found something familiar about Fari'a's irrigated soil. Although the old men would always find life in the mountains incongruous, the watered fields gave them

Fari'a camp.

hope of a temporary livelihood and offered them something to fasten their dreams onto. Abu Tarik wistfully remembers a pool near his home in Al-Kafrein being watered from a horse-drawn well; he recalls a scene so beautiful that people came from considerable distances to watch the operation. Abu Mustafa arrived in 1952 and was one of the few who had the resources to take a farm tenancy nearby. Another of the fortunate few, a man who had acquired some dry land elsewhere, went in search of somewhere more fertile. His search ended when he saw people taking water from Fari'a spring. For these two men the water denoted fertile land, for the parents of the future camp official it denoted farm work.

The early camp was an unprepossessing sight. Abu Tarik's first impression in 1951 was of 100 tents scattered widely across the valley slopes. Canvas offered scant protection against the plummeting temperatures and sweeping gales of winter; some tents were blown away in these first years. Their capacity varied according to the size of family using them, and this grew rapidly after the first year. Soon the passageways between them began to shrink as more and larger tents were needed. Small blockhouses started to supplant them in 1956, families of eight or more receiving larger ones. Families survived by stretching and sharing their bare rations supplied by the Red Cross and the UN body set up to provide for the refugees – The United Nations' Relief and Works Agency for Refugees in the Near East (UNRWA). Other resources were got wherever they could be found. Abu Tarik worked on a local farm for five piastres a day, out of which he eventually saved enough to buy a donkey. He then began to sell vegetables in nearby villages. Women went into the fields when their clan custom allowed, working for half the male rate. Abu Fathi took up the trade of shoemaker, which his uncle had taught him back in Al-Kafrein. When his uncle fled hurriedly in 1948, Abu Fathi took the abandoned equipment, thinking it might become useful. He remembers each of his fellow wanderers receiving four kilos of flour every ten days (and some milk and potatoes from the Red Cross) in Jericho about 1950. Wild flowers and berries were a vital supplement. Soon he moved to Ramallah where the flour ration rose slightly to 14 kilos a month. In the early 1950s UNRWA began providing milk and other drinks for schoolboys, and an assortment of clothes for all children. It now became possible for families to budget for small, temporary surpluses of food.

A remarkable continuity of social organisation linked the last years of life in the villages with the early years in the camp. This achievement defied the sheer scale of human chaos after 1947. Some of the more prominent differences between clans must have made co-existence irksome and distasteful. The ubiquitous poverty acted as a social solvent by driving workers some distance away from their homes. Women went into the fields to work while men went looking for work in nearby Nablus or distant Beirut. Female refugees encountered new social rules, for women in the Nablus-Fari'a area were traditionally more likely to work outside the home than women anywhere else in old Palestine. Many villages did not approve of women working outside the home at all. In 1948 some villages would not allow their women to marry outsiders; one village sustained this custom until 1967. Separatism was probably taken to its greatest height by one Fari'a clan, which, one man remembers, still functioned as a tight community into the 1960s. But even though people came to Fari'a from many scattered points of old Palestine, they all expected to return there once the fighting was over and things had settled down. The small size of the camp probably helped to keep divisive issues down to a manageable, human scale. Also, although poverty might have divided people it also had the effect of drawing them together – the first families to arrive depended on handouts from the only well-off man among them. The status quo was supported by UNRWA: its local officials were generally Palestinian refugees and they sided with existing forms of authority; officials were forbidden to get involved in politics. Moreover, the conservative and co-operative traditions of a rural people were deeply engrained. Despite the physical disorder of the camp's early days, strong traditions of deference to the leading families and of cooperation within each clan eased the camp past incipient signs of discontent. Each clan and village cherished the distinctiveness of their identity and customs, and they also respected each other's.

The administration of this community of many strangers fell into place quickly. The senior men of the leading families met and sorted out contentious issues and, replicating the system that existed in each clan, they appointed a leader (mukhtar) of the whole camp and backed up his authority. In addition, an 18-man Camp Committee was formed quickly to work with the mukhtar and to negotiate with the Jordanian Government, who had emerged from the fighting as the de facto controller of the West Bank. The Jordanians had no intention of altering things; they were fellow Arabs of a conservative disposition, concerned only that the Palestinians did not create a separate focus of power within their own state. On day-to-day issues the UNRWA officials worked hand-in-hand with the elders. The camp was fortunate in possessing many experienced leaders. Five of the seven notables chosen for the committee had been leaders of pre-1948 villages. Other committee members were chosen for their ability to contribute to decisions in ways that rose above the narrow interests of their village of origin. Social relations in the mid-1950s were 'supportive, tight and respectful,' said a present-day camp official. This harmonious state of affairs owed itself to a quite astonishing ability to adapt old traditions to the needs of survival.

The camp was still putting its house in order when it was rocked by the shock of momentous external movements. Anger had already been expressed against the Jordanian authorities as early as 1951 for failing to pressure Israel over the refugee issue. The price paid for this precocious and insubordinate behaviour, in contrast to the silence in the larger and less uniform Balata camp in Nablus, was a collective fine. Soon political demonstrations swept through an Arab world that, in the early 1950s, believed the western powers were trying to dominate the region's political agendas. Communist, Baathist and other parties appeared. These activities found a counterpart in the camp. An old activist remembers the politicisation of these years with pride, but a camp official saw this at the time, rightly although prematurely, as a threat to some aspects of traditional Arab authority. He approved of the speed with which the Jordanians nipped the nascent political organisations in the bud. These were the first of many increasingly severe challenges to an authority structure that the camp had swiftly and carefully erected after the shock of 1948. The politicised young men of Fari'a resorted to direct action in the late 1960s, at a time when the Palestinian Liberation Organisation (PLO), itself only formed in 1964, began to enjoy a growing appeal in the West Bank. With young men from other refugee camps, Fari'a's fedayeen (irregular fighters) made raids across the Israeli border. In one raid a youth was killed when the Israelis retaliated. The camp was a better recruiting ground for the PLO thereafter. The camp's residents wanted to return to their farms in the state of Israel and, after years of international inaction, they were beginning to feel that fighting was the only way to reclaim it.

Slowly, material conditions eased. A few men displayed a singular ability to develop their capacities and to lessen the dependence of their families on UNRWA aid. They were out of the ordinary. One is Abu Tarik who was a young, recently married man in 1948. He put money aside from farm wages and became a hawker. His profits from collecting goods in Nablus and selling them in villages near the camp rose from 25 to 50 piastres a day during the 1950s. Noticing that it was getting cheaper to obtain goods from Nablus in the 1960s he rented a shop in the camp to supplement his other outlets. By now he had 10 children, only five being eligible for UNRWA relief. It was necessary for his wife to take over the shop while he went on his rounds. Even this modest success story had its periods of panic and un-predictability. Jordanian military service took him away from home for a few months soon after he acquired the shop. His brother helped in the shop and lent him five dinars a week, until his own marriage in 1967 cut off this lifeline. The disruption of the 1967 War, in which many camp fedayeen fought against Israel before fleeing to Jordan, closed the shop down for three months. Only when his eldest son found work about 1968 did the family's income recover. By contrast, a camp official took the educational route to a more assured professional career. He completed his fourth secondary grade by walking a round trip of 30 kilometres northwest each day to a Jenin school. Vocational training followed, leading to a post as a mechanical engineer at a water plant when he was 19. Promotions rapidly followed until, aged 36, he took over at Fari'a in 1976. Both men used their abilities and hard work to take advantage of slowly improving conditions, but both were exceptional.

Israeli victory and occupation in 1967 did more to change and radicalise camp society than all earlier developments. An army of occupation took up position and Israeli martial law was imposed. Israeli settlements began to rise on hilltops near Arab communities. Everyone in the camp looked at these developments in horror; they also felt the loss of prominent families who fled to Jordan to avoid Israeli reprisals after the 1967 War. The initial effect, as everyone began to recover from the shock of occupation, was to draw people together. Paradoxically, a much greater threat to solidarity came later, when the relatively well-paid Israeli job market, responding to a post-war economic boom, was opened to the camp's young people. Some of the youth became disenchanted with traditional mores as a result and the camp's leaders were at a loss how to act. The power of tradition did not stretch across the 'Green Line' (the 1948 border with Israel): six cases of promiscuity were alleged among the 80 or so women working there; a number of young men were believed to have become drunk or unruly. This behaviour was deeply offensive to Muslims. At the same time, more women went to work in the fields in the 1970s as clan proscriptions were ignored. The dismay of the traditionalists was compounded in the early 1970s when the Israelis replaced a popular mukhtar with a collaborator who quickly imposed his will on the camp committee. Whereas the ideas of Arab intellectuals, back in the 1950s, had no far-reaching effect on society in Fari'a, the identifiable moral lapses of the late 1960s did. The intellectuals had called for a new Arab world order and had held Israel up as an outpost of western ideology. Their debates had directed intellectual attention to the world stage. Although these ideas would soon constitute a challenge to traditional Arab society in Egypt, Syria and Iraq, they could not be established in the West Bank while the Jordanian army policed these developments so well. The appeal of the PLO in the camp was weak before the early 1970s. The camp was therefore insulated from external influences that might pose a threat to tradition. By contrast, the exposure of Fari'a youth to new attitudes to sex and the use of narcotics in Israel from 1967 caused a decay of cultural and moral beliefs from inside the camp itself. The flight of some families to Jordan was soon followed by another migration, this time westwards, as those with jobs in Israel moved nearer to their work. The shrinkage in numbers was nothing compared to the acute strain that these depredations put on the clan and village system. One clan was amazed to see four men competing for the leadership of their community, a position that had hitherto been filled by the acclaim of the elders. Allegiance to some smaller clan and village communities withered away altogether.

The Israeli occupation posed a brutal dilemma. It put the destiny of the camp into the hands of the hated power that had destroyed or depopulated many villages during the fighting, yet it offered well-paid work, something that was unimaginable under Jordanian rule. Discontent with the new masters reached a point in the early 1970s where the camp could not avoid making a choice between its economic well-being on the one hand and its religious and moral values and national consciousness on the other. In 1971 the Israelis gave the collaborator-mukhtar power to decide who should work in three Israeli factories where some 200 Fari'a men were employed. At the same time the PLO was recruiting vigorously. The tug of war between groups supporting the mukhtar and the PLO had the effect of rapidly politicising the young men. Fari'a's unity fell apart. Two thirds of the camp stayed loyal to the mukhtar because – so one man remembers – of his powers of patronage. Opposition to the mukhtar met with harassment by Israeli troops, often followed by imprisonment. Most men kept quiet or collaborated; those who spoke out usually found themselves in an Israeli prison. The camp committee was tainted by its subservience to the mukhtar. Fears of betrayal and reprisal swept through the camp. In retrospect, it is easy to see the developments of these years proceeding with a dogged inevitability. The many young Palestinian prisoners converted the Israeli gaols into political seminaries. If a prisoner was not already 'turned' by the Israelis, he became a political radical who spurned the authority of his own traditional leaders on his release. The Israelis had tried to control the situation by pulling simultaneously both the traditional and the modern levers of power – the position of the mukhtar in Arab society and the Israeli job market. Within a decade the effect of Israeli occupation was to breed an assertive political awareness among the young men that threatened both to topple Israeli power and to destabilise local society. Divisions of interest and factional mistrust began fatally to undermine the social cohesion and respect for traditional authority so carefully built up among Palestinians since 1950. The social divisions that opened up during the popular uprising (or intifada) against the Israeli occupation that lasted from 1987 to 1993 followed fault-lines already established in the preceding 20 years.

In material terms, the years following the Occupation were a golden age. Virtually every man with a travel pass and skills or strength worked in Israel or the Gulf (and other Arab States). Some men had managed to find work in Beirut back in the 1950s, others in Germany and the Gulf in the 1960s. But 1968 heralded a change in the order of things. About 900 Fari'a men, 80% of those of working age, worked in Israel between 1968 and the outbreak of the intifada in 1987, according to one source. This work was mostly unskilled labouring. Those with 12th school grade or over were attracted by skilled jobs in the Gulf. Estimates of the number of cheques entering the camp every month vary between 40 and 60; Sheikh Walaa guessed that their value was on average between 30 and 100 JD (£30-£100). Abu Tarik believed that three-quarters of all families benefited at some time or other. The number of remittances depended on how well a family was endowed with sons, and the income fell away when the sons married. Nonetheless, the effect of remittances and high Israeli wages began to show itself in the many repairs to the small and decaying UNRWA blockhouses, now well over a decade old. Extra floors pushed the houses upwards and transformed the Fari'a skyline.

The intifada erupted in December 1987. The old cohesion had survived in flashes until then, for example when virtually the whole camp turned out in 1986 to demonstrate against the failure of the Arab Conciliation Summit to address the Palestinian issue. Although the PLO-Israeli battle of Al-Karemeh ended indecisively in the same year, the Palestinians claimed victory, and Fari'a refugees publicly expressed their joy even though it was believed that collaborators would point them out to the Israeli authorities. But factions had already appeared in Fari'a in 1982, and their appeal quickly cut across loyalty to the clans. At this point the factions co-operated with each other, however. Though not part of the PLO, Islamist groups worked with the factions. More disturbing however, the ill-disciplined young men, intoxicated with a sense of power, stopped buses of workers leaving for Israel and closed schools. The collapse of clan and village authority, though each possessed its particular history of decline, was rapid after 1982. Before then, the camp director would confer with the old 'wise men' when disturbances threatened; he expected the youth to obey their elders. Thereafter the young men took no special heed of his or the old men's words.

Unarmed civilians took a lead from the refugees and rose as one throughout the West Bank in December 1987. They refused to accept the writ and power of the Israeli army. Initially, in the words of shrewd observers, 'a rebellion of the poor...powered by the hardship of getting through each day, not the hope for a brighter political future',[1] the intifada spontaneously developed into an expression of rage against foreign domination. Rabin, the Israeli Defence Minister, and Arafat, the PLO leader in distant Tunis, were both taken by surprise. People broke curfews, waved the red, green and black Palestinian flag (punishable by imprisonment) and stood in the street in front of Israeli soldiers daring them to do their worst.

The mood in the camp lifted; resilience was palpable for a few short months. The collaborator-mukhtar was chased away and informers were rooted out by the simple method of watching for those who avoided the celebrations. Corruption was halted as the culprits were caught and punished. People spoke together in groups and shared food during curfews. Ironically, workers were still wanted in Israel, which was experiencing an economic boom. According to one source, almost as many men of working age found jobs in Israel, the Gulf or elsewhere throughout the intifada as had been the case in the previous decade. Committees were formed to coordinate the resistance over a wide area. They reduced the lingering resentment of the indigenous population to the refugees and united everyone in the national cause. An awareness of the sacrifices of life, health and livelihood that everyone was undergoing smoothed relations between camp dwellers and neighbouring villagers and townspeople.

Euphoria was short-lived, however. Within six months the camp entered new psychological territory as it grappled with the prospect of fragmentation. Ironically, although no one knew at the time, the intifada had already won a major victory: Rabin admitted the Israelis could not defeat it but were indeed fighting only to contain it. In Fari'a however, chaos began to spread. Even now, some residents believe the deep internal divisions that appeared early in the intifada were only an intensification of the squabbles that preceded it while others feel that something radically new was happening. An official characterised the intifada as a time of

---

(1) Ze'ev Schiff and Ehud Ya'ari, *Intifada. The Palestinian Uprising – Israel's Third Front* (New York, Touchstone, 1991) pp 79-80.

'politicisation, assertiveness, uncertainty and poverty.' The sharing of food smuggled into the camp stopped. Each faction began to look after its own members. Young men burned down their own clubhouse. An un-related stabbing of a youth has reverberations even today. Rumours spread that the Israelis had learned the names of activists from a youth in gaol. The use of masks by some young men struck at the heart of the Arab desire to see whom he is addressing. The Arab yearning for social interaction went unfulfilled in the many curfews (one in 1989 lasted 90 days, another 75 days).

The young men were now firmly in control. Hitherto the camp committee had drawn its inspiration from traditional values. It had deferred to the views of the mukhtar. Power now passed to the newly formed youth committees for education, health, agriculture and conciliation; others were created as the need arose. The four chief factions – Fatah, Hamas,[1] the Communists and the Democratic Front – came together to distribute external aid to the most needy families. The clans attracted antagonism. No traditional leaders were recognised. When a clan member was injured he had to seek help from a faction; belonging to one was now essential.

On my first visit to Fari'a in November 1995 the heavy reliance of organised life on the initiative and participation of Fatah was striking. In the early 1990s this faction claimed that its dominant appeal, located in the mainstream of politics, gave it the only legitimate right to appoint people to committees, where in any case it generally secured a majority. Its strength is epitomised by its command of 550 of the 900 votes on the UNRWA Youth Club committee in 1996. The remaining votes were shared between the Communists, Hamas, Popular Front and Democratic Front. The mosque committee operated without division, being concerned only with the un-contentious issue of the building of a new mosque but, in any case, two-thirds of its members were affiliated to Fatah in 1996.

---

(1) Fatah is an acronym in Arabic of The Movement for the National Liberation of Palestine. The largest group within the PLO, it is led by Arafat. Since 1988 it has accepted the State of Israel. Hamas is an acronym of the leading militant Islamic group. Formed in 1988, it rejects the State of Israel.

The establishment of Hamas in the camp by 1990 boosted traditional (both Islamic and Arab) authority and values. It also added to the political tension. By seeking the destruction of Israel, Hamas represented a clear political alternative to Fatah's mainstream position. The loyalty of many families was now split between factions. A sour joke of the time referred to 'one family, three parts.' Parental authority was sometimes challenged, an unheard-of development in Arab mores. A case, recounted to me as typical of the disarray of the times, concerned a boy who threatened to report his father to his faction if he were not allowed to go to a demonstration. Social relations had become dry and un-nourishing. As Sheikh Walaa emphasised, it was not only political divisions that kept people apart, 'inequitable distribution and bad feelings were the thing.' On the other hand, some families had always sought to heal their internal divisions; scattered acts of reconciliation had probably become the norm by the middle of the 1990s. One young Islamist from an otherwise Fatah family explained how factional support and religious devotion could be reconciled when families placed emphasis on their mutual respect and the common base of their Muslim faith. This young man was also convinced that the smallness of the camp kept disagreements down to a manageable human scale.

The young men now loosened their grip. The original camp and mosque committees quickly began to return to their former significance. This was hardly a sweeping change though, and it owed as much to dismay with inter-factional wrangling as to the appeal of the older system. Clan leaders have generally avoided involvement in political issues, yet they were, and still are, consulted about the choice of candidates for elections to committees, a benign intermingling of the two hitherto antagonistic forms of allegiance. The largest villages of origin, Al-Kafrein and Um Al-Zianat, which account for some 60% of the camp, have created their own social co-ordinating committees. Al-Kafrein has the largest number of 'village seats' on the camp committee – four of the nine. People from Al-Kafrein and another village, Sawalima, still co-operate and consult on important matters. Abu Fathi believes that the youth cooperate well with the conservatives on the camp committee and that, on major issues, this committee now has the support of the whole camp. Its ability to rise above factional interests is exemplified in a recent case recounted by Sheikh Walaa. The factions made claims on the house of a woman who died intestate. Hamas wanted to make it the home of a religious sheikh; Fatah wanted it as an office; the communists favoured it as a library. The committee overruled all these claims, sold the house and spent the proceeds for the benefit of everyone in the camp. The cooperative assumptions of clan society might be detected behind this decision. Nonetheless, Abdel Massih, a leader in one of the factions, believes the clans and villages have had their day. He attributes the smooth running of the committees, firmly based now on pluralistic principles, to the responsibility shown by the youth and the factions. He acknowledges the reconciliation achieved by old clan leaders and the youth, yet he returns to what is for him clearly a rhetorical question, 'How can my clan or village help me when I turn to my faction for important things now?'

The ascendancy of the factions might indeed be irrevocable. This might be one route modernity is taking in the West Bank and Gaza. Yet the resilience of old allegiances in a community that has been exposed to strong and strident ideological claims is remarkable. It may only be a counterpoint to factional power now, but the co-operative nature of clan and village life still finds a purpose. It offers balm to the many, deep wounds inflicted by the rapid introduction of a modern political consciousness and acts as a restorative for the exhaustion resulting from military harassment in the 1980s and crippling unemployment in the 1990s. The coming together of the whole camp for weddings and funerals today is recognition of these lingering centrifugal tendencies. They only linger, however; they have little dynamic power. Their purpose remains that of helping to hold things together. The future might lie in an exploration of the infant relationship between the bruised and mutually suspicious clans and factions. Into this picture has been thrown an internationally-brokered peace process. It promises to look at the position of the refugees. As they wait for the process to unfold many Fari'a residents are worried they may be ignored.

* * *

The bus pulled into West Jerusalem Bus Station and I went in search of another one to take me across the town. More than half the people around me are in military uniform. I have no illusions about the situation I'm entering. The Palestinians are resisting a military occupation. Years later, this moment at the end of 1995 would be seen as a high water mark in the Peace Process that is grappling with this issue.[1] The process began in Oslo two years earlier. Oslo Stage One gave the Palestinians partial autonomy in Jericho and in Gaza; now Oslo Two is due, in which Israeli soldiers will leave the other towns they occupied in 1967 (including Nablus, but excluding Hebron where a small influx of Jewish settlers has altered the political geography of the town). In addition, a release of Palestinian prisoners has been agreed. The truly prickly issues like the right of Palestinian refugees to return to their homeland and the claims of the Palestinians to Jerusalem as their capital have been left to 'final status' talks five years hence. Oslo Two is proceeding more or less to plan although Israel is delaying the release of some prisoners. But the distress and belligerence shown in the utterances of both sides keeps everyone on tenterhooks. Suspicion, distrust and obloquy flourish and seem destined to interfere with the process. Yitzhak Rabin, the Israeli Prime Minister, has to take account of Israeli fears of annihilation and to tread very warily with the Israeli extreme Right. The Palestinians have so far gained little of substance after two years of a peace process that offered hope of independence and of an amelioration of their poor economic conditions. Anger in the West Bank and Gaza over Israel's failure to keep to the schedule of prisoner releases has just erupted in violence. Israel has retaliated by imposing what she calls a 'closure' two weeks before I arrived. This means that Israeli soldiers are preventing anyone moving from their town or village, even for the most urgent of reasons.

Moreover, many thousands of Palestinians have recently been expelled from the Gulf States, in a fall-out from the Gulf War. When Saddam Hussein threatened Kuwait the Palestinians sided with Iraq because Hussein coincidentally called for the liberation of the Palestinians. Kuwait and Saudi Arabia are now paying the Palestinians back for supporting Iraq. They have for long kept the PLO in funds; inevitably they have now stopped this flow, and the PLO is believed to be almost bankrupt. The Palestinians are paying dearly for their popular support of Iraq. On top of all this, Colonel Gaddafy has just begun to expel Palestinians from Libya, apparently as an expression of anger against Arafat for acquiescing in a one-sided peace process with Israel. The large expulsion of

---

(1) Graham Usher, *Dispatches from Palestine: The Rise and Fall of the Oslo Peace Process* (London, Pluto Press, 1999) p 53.

Palestinians from unsympathetic Arab states has added to the already ferocious levels of unemployment in the West Bank and Gaza. Refugee services are in crisis. High birth rates and widespread poverty amongst Palestinian refugees are putting pressure on the funds the United Nations allocates to their welfare. Some countries are not paying their UN dues. Events in my town of destination, Nablus, are reflecting the wider turmoil. Armed Israeli settlers have taken over the shrine of Joseph's Tomb on the edge of the town. The Israeli army is about to demolish the homes near Nablus of two men accused of taking part in a bombing earlier in the year. One home is in a refugee camp. In response, the residents of the camp have called a general strike. If this is an optimistic time in the peace process it provokes all the heart-stopping emotions of defeat too.

* * *

I left the urban bus before it reached East Jerusalem. I was afraid it might veer away from my route and was too embarrassed to clarify this with the preoccupied-looking driver, in charge of a full bus. In any case, Israeli buses venture only to the edge of East Jerusalem where I have to find the Arab bus station. I was able to indulge my desire to be among people at the price of greater discomfort in the soaring temperature. It was 75 degrees, un-seasonally hot for late October. I hauled my cases along Jaffa Road and past the modernistic Municipal Offices. Now the street dipped down into Arab East Jerusalem and the congested humanity that is Damascus Gate and Salah al-din Street. The environment was immediately transformed. I had left the West behind and entered the Orient. I recognised no Jews now; there was hardly a white or near-white skin in sight. Crowds of Arabs overflowed the pavements; car horns bewailed this trespass on their space. Taxi drivers shouted, 'Ramallah!', 'Nablus!' Fruit and vegetables covered most of the pavement outside the Damascus Gate of the Old City and their vendors approached anyone who showed the slightest interest. I wandered away from the Gate looking for the bus station. Street life and buildings here seem of an earlier age and, at a mundane level, I noticed the potholes that have appeared in the street since I left the Jewish part of the city. People moved at a different pace from a few hundred yards to the west. I was bemused by the strange tempo and the hubbub of Arabic voices and the variety and blend of food smells that filled the air.

CHAPTER 3

Nablus, October 1995

Climbing geraniums, freesias, hibiscus. Plumbago in bundles of blue on dressed stone walls. The terraces look spell-bound in the clear sun. Nablus is pretty, it is close, on a scale of intimacy.

David Pryce-Jones

THIS CONGESTION OF emotions and thoughts accompanied me to Ramallah, where I found the Nablus bus. Very slowly it began to fill with passengers as the time for departure came and passed. Long minutes crept by. I begin to feel the bus would remain firmly berthed here, its driver chatting with friends. I asked again when we would leave, only to be told, sympathetically, that we must of course wait for the bus to fill up before we go on. This is my first lesson in cultural adjustment, something to do with the relation between time and people, certainly a questioning of priorities. I realised that, whether because of cultural shyness or my natural reserve, I was sitting some way behind the small groups of Arabs already on the bus. In any case, as they boarded, the other passengers showed only mild interest in me. The dusty torn jeans, faded shirt and weather-beaten face of one man suggested he had come straight from some labouring work. An old couple in traditional dress talked together quietly and supportively all the way. Most others looked out of the window or dozed. Hills were soon all around us. After a talkative 30 minutes the driver subsided into a silent attentiveness to the potholed road and the villagers walking along the sandy verges. Labouring badly on the steeper slopes the bus followed a noisy path along the weaving hilly road, stopping at isolated farmhouses and anonymous side roads. About half way the driver pulled up outside a dilapidated, lean-to garage and disappeared into the back for about 10 minutes. He emerged, Pepsi can in hand, and directed a burst of guffaws and farewells to his invisible friends. In the early afternoon we enter the outskirts – ramshackle to my western eyes – of Nablus; so many new unoccupied shops and extempore garages along the road. I am the last to step from the bus into the dusty brightness of Al-Hussein Square. The first person I asked for directions to the university was a student there, Rishou. My query in Arabic soon became a conversation in English while he persuaded his friend to give me a lift up the lower slopes of Mt Gerizim to the university. He summarised his views on life in the West Bank on the short journey, adding, with disgust, that he has to sell cigarettes, smuggled through Israel I think, in order to pay his college fees – there is so little work available. A rushed introduction to Khalil in my fragmented state of awareness – thank heaven the university surroundings look familiar. I have just time to register a small, moustachioed, extremely polite and exact man in his fifties – before he takes me down into the town centre again to my apartment.

Now Nablus monopolises my senses. My first impression is of milling crowds – a confabulation of people – talking on the congested roads, treating the public space with the familiarity of the home and moving around as if everyone is joined in one public expression of humanity, rejecting individualism. Bright light and warm air touch my eyes and skin, staccato sounds of car horns assail my ears, the smell of spicy food drifting across the downtown air tantalises my nose. The curious looks of people make me conscious that, other than the occasional journalist or aid worker, Europeans have rarely been seen here for a decade. I am an object of curiosity as well as an observer.

The town was a provincial centre of the Ottoman Empire and British Mandate. It was once a walled city, possessing 9 gates, of which one remains. The last besieging army surrounded these walls in 1771 when 12,000 riflemen were believed to have assembled in its defence. The Ottoman Pasha of Sidon, Zahir al-Umar, who was responsible for this part of Palestine, wanted to impose his authority on this rich inland merchant city and its hinterland. After nine days of skirmishes and a major battle he withdrew. The town's last

NABLUS OLD CITY

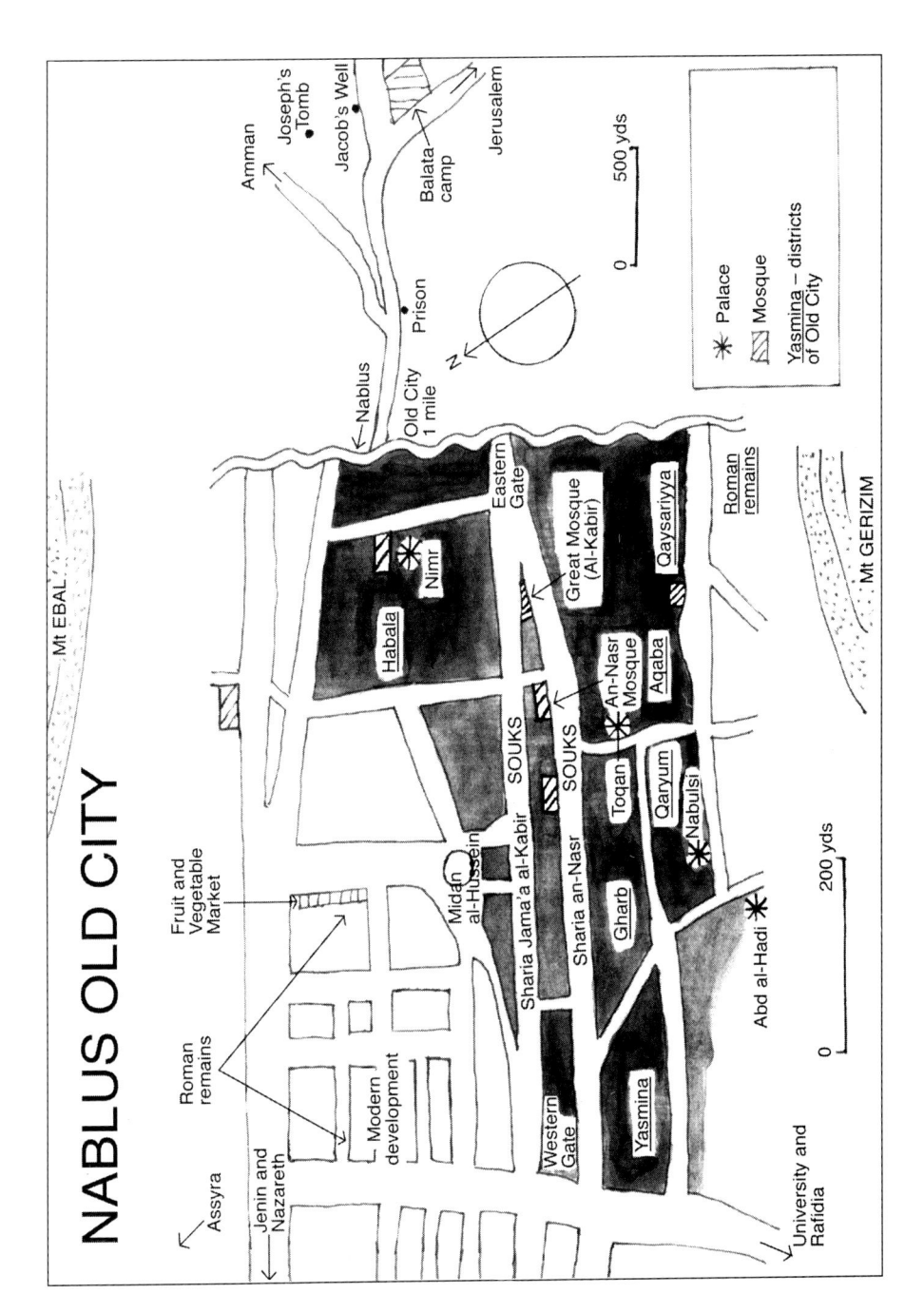

military engagement before this century, when the forces of the ambitious Ottoman Governor of Egypt, Muhammad Ali, were at its gates in 1834, ended without a blow being struck after one of Nablus' patrician families offered to negotiate. The town's commercial development has benefited from its position astride trade routes between Beirut, Cairo, Damascus and Jerusalem. It owes its reputation as a beautiful and fertile spot ('a palace in a garden') to its location above a large number of natural springs. It possesses a proud cluster of grand palaces and imposing town houses belonging to the big families, Nabulsis, Toqans, Abd al-Hadis and Nimrs, names that have represented power secure in their hilly fastness over the centuries, families who had long spurned

Nablus. Old City wall. Welding workshop on right.

the orders of distant Ottoman rulers. Their stone-built residences, alongside the smaller houses of lesser burgesses, are huddled tightly together for protection in and around the Old City. The ground floors were once given over to stables, storage, schools and servants' quarters. The upper floors were the family's domain, under the strict control of the women of the family. The rooms were large and splendid and had dome-shaped ceilings in obedience to Ottoman taste of the 18th and 19th centuries. Most peasants must have been impressed by the tall three- and four-storied residential buildings, if only because they reminded them of the grand compounds of their sub-district chiefs.'[1]

This orderly world was destroyed in the summer of 1927 when an earthquake devastated the town. The tremor might have been no more serious here than anywhere else along the north-south axis it affected, but the old and fragile buildings of central Nablus could not withstand it. Seventy dead were found immediately but many more bodies remained in the ruins. Two observers, on the spot soon afterwards, reported that 'earthquake damage [in Nablus] was the most serious in the country, and many people were killed...It's a pitiful sight. In the main bazaar the houses, all three storeys high, collapsed. As every room seems to have been built and owned by a different person, this has produced insoluble problems in the rebuilding. All the houses lean against each other, and even now, when they touch a dividing wall, there are more collapses and three more have recently been killed. We mountaineered over piles of rubble on to any roofs left standing.'[2]

Only the Old City (il qadime) still offers a glimpse of the glories that today's grandparents took for granted. It huddles behind stretches of wall, 40 feet high in places and encloses the souks, which are narrow streets and alleys filled with shops, cafes, bakeries and metal and other workshops, and one of the five small factories making olive oil soap by traditional methods, for which the town

---

(1) Beshara Doumani, *Rediscovering Palestine: Merchants and Peasants in Jabal Nablus, 1700-1900* (London, 1995) p27.
(2) Norman and Helen Bentwich, *Mandate Memories, 1918-1948* (London, 1965) p 115. See also Eunice Holliday, *Letters from Jerusalem during the Palestine Mandate* (ed. John C Holliday) (London, Radcliffe Press, 1997) pp74-75.

is still famous. Intermingled with this busy, small-scale world are the ancient residencies of town leaders. The large rambling palaces of old patrician families are surrounded by tranquil, tree-filled gardens. The Old City and its environs are now an area of social extremes, poor unskilled labourers for the main part living a short distance from the town's leading families. In the rock of the wall itself homes have been carved, some of the highest possessing ancient gardens built on rock ledges. Plants, bushes and small trees create the illusion of a lofty Arcadian world, disturbed only by sounds from the busy souks below. The area of the souks is smaller than the famous one in the Old City of Jerusalem, but it is more tightly integrated into the life of the town. Nablus lost its tourist trade during the intifada ('shaking free' in Arabic), a popular uprising against the Israeli occupation that ended a few years ago. Its reputation for revolt – 'the most anti-Zionist and anti-British Arabs of Nablus – which is always a hot-bed of Arab discontent', said the wife of the Legal Secretary to the Mandate authority in the early 1920s[1] – and the Israeli authorities' policy of dissuading tourists from going into the West Bank have kept tourists away. In this town of between 125,000 and 150,000 people, the biggest on the West Bank, there is only one substantial hotel. Elsewhere in the town a few old houses remain in otherwise new streets. For the rest, the town is modern, although traditional in style. Its abiding glory is not its architecture, however, but its location. It fills the valley between (and climbs the slopes of) Mt Gerizim and Mt Ebal, of Biblical fame. The swift sunrise over Ebal and sunset over the edge of Gerizim define the Nablus day.

The big families don't have the political power they once enjoyed. Arafat and the new political elite have taken it over. But at a local level the traditional leaders still count for much and they control considerable wealth. Arafat is wooing them in order to build a broad social coalition of support for his policies. This is contributing to tension in the town between rich and poor, because the refugees in surrounding camps feel their case has been unheeded in political counsels since the Oslo process began. The refugees have never felt fully accepted by the people of this hill town since they found their way here in 1948.

---

(1) *Ibid*, p 90.

The refugees are the last of a long line of people to settle here. A mile or so south east of today's city centre, next to Balata refugee camp, a Chalcolithic town was in being about 4,000 BC. On the same site, some 2,100 years later, another town, Shekhem, was established. Built by Canaanites, it was a powerful city-state when, the Bible tells us, Abraham was sent here by God to claim the Promised Land of Israel. It was here in Shekhem that he and his grandson Jacob built altars to God. After the Israelite conquest of Canaan Joshua assembled the victorious tribes of Israel here and affirmed the Covenant with Yahweh. Jacob bought land locally; Joseph is buried here. In Shekhem the Israelites revolted against the taxes imposed by Solomon and declared a separate state, the 'northern kingdom', under King Jeroboam 1. The Samaritans strengthened their ties to the area around Shekhem by building a temple on Mt Gerizim, in opposition to the Jews of Jerusalem. But, in the 9th Century BC, King Omri moved the northern capital to Samaria a few miles away, a decision that caused Shekhem to decline. A century later an army of southern Jews sacked Shekhem and destroyed the Samaritan Temple on Gerizim, laying the whole area to waste. Shekhem never recovered. Only when the Romans built another new town (Neapolis), shortly after the Samaritan revolt of 72 AD, a couple of miles further north along the pass between the two mountains, on what is now Nablus, did urban life flourish here again. The Roman settlement, on the site of a Samaritan village, was built for the veterans of Titus' campaigns only a few years after the collapse of the Samaritan revolt against the Romans. It is possible that its purpose was to make sure there was not another rising of the Samaritans. The remains of Roman Neapolis are in abundance in Nablus today – a theatre (able to seat between 6,000 and 7,000 people, excavations reveal) and a hippodrome some 300 yards away. The Arabs took Neapolis in 636 AD and gave it its modern Arabic name of Nablus. They lost possession for about 90 years when the Crusaders captured it in 1099. During that time the Crusaders built a fortress on the top of Mt Gerizim and a number of churches in the town, one of which stood at the centre of the Old City and was dedicated to John the Baptist who baptised people in the springs nearby. This church was also said to be on the spot where Joseph's brothers presented Jacob with the bloodstained coat of many colours to persuade him his favourite son was dead. After Saladin won the town back for the Arabs in

1187 Nablus' Great Mosque was raised on this site. Today, little remains above ground of these religious artefacts. Only Joseph's Tomb and the Byzantine convent at Jacob's Well escaped the effects of the 1927 earthquake and the rapacious desire of earlier inhabitants for building stones.

I never saw the Tomb, perhaps because it was a little off my route to Balata camp, perhaps because I was already saturated with the sight of troops. However, Jacob's Well is only across the road from Balata, behind the anonymity of a solid high wall and gate, and I went one day. St John's Gospel tells of a Samaritan woman coming to collect water from where Jesus, whom she identifies as a Jew, was resting by the well. Jesus was on his way to the Galilee in flight from the Jewish authorities in Judea. The dialogue is intriguing; the bitter alienation between the Jerusalem and Samaritan versions of Judaism hovers in the air. Although the Jerusalem Jews had destroyed the Samaritan Temple on Mt Gerizim and brutally imposed a Jerusalem version of Judaism on the dissident Samaritans more than a century before, the memory of this event was still vivid when Jesus met the Samaritan woman.[1] An almost theatrical fencing with words occurs when Jesus mentions the 'living water' of God, as if the woman senses the truth of his deeper identity but needs to approach it slowly (John, 4). The scriptural significance of this encounter cannot be overstated: one authority has said that 'if we leave out the apostles, [the woman of the well] is, after Mary at Cana, the first genuine believer.'[2] The well is a beautiful place, full of brooding history. Inside the high stonewalls, large slabs decorated with Eastern Orthodox Christian symbols lie scattered about the entrance to the well, as if some great force were holding back the completion of the shrine, which looks a simple matter now. The priest's house, surrounded by trellises of vines and flowers, is a picture of tranquillity, even though recent events have the power to erode its calm. After threats from Israeli settlers the priest was killed at the entrance to the shrine a few years ago. Maybe this is why the restoration is in limbo, maybe it is for

---

(1) Jerome Murphy-O'Connor, *The Holy Land. An Oxford Archaeological Guide from Earliest Times to 1700* (Oxford, 1998) p372.
(2) Herman Servotte, *According to John: Literary Reading of the Fourth Gospel* (London, 1994) p 24.

lack of money. In any case, there is something doleful in the air despite the heat of the day.

All the other work of the Crusaders and Eastern Orthodox Churches was swept away. The Russian and Greek Orthodox Churches have made a number of attempts to rebuild the shrine at Jacob's Well; the latter administer it still. The survival of Biblical remains alongside the human evidence of today's political travails in Nablus' eastern suburbs is breathtaking. Balata refugee camp lies next to the site of Shekhem. Joseph's Tomb, a short distance away, is occupied by Israeli troops. Jacob's Well, lying almost opposite the main entrance to the refugee camp, still shows the scars of a hand grenade explosion that killed the priest. Israeli troops, Orthodox priests and Palestinian refugees live within 100 yards of each other. Overlooking this intensely religious place is Mt Gerizim, which is important to Jews, Samaritans, Christians and Muslims: a common ancestry and common cause of apprehension.

Richard Crossman, a future British Labour Minister, an enthusiastic Zionist and a member of the Anglo-American Enquiry Commission for Palestine, was taken to the top of the mountain one night in 1946 by Arab notables from Nablus and shown the lights of surrounding Jewish settlements in an effort to convey to him their fears of Jewish immigration. His thoughts took another direction, however, reflecting the insecurity that seems to have dogged each wave of occupiers of this land. 'He understood how, 3,000 years ago, the Children of Israel, whose chief town was then Shekhem, on that very site where he was standing, felt when they looked down on the coastal plain occupied by the camps of the Philistines, who had come from over the sea with their iron chariots and threatened the Israelite homes in the hills.'[1]

I could find little physical evidence of the British presence in Nablus under the Mandate. Near one entrance to the souks an old road sign is in English as well as Arabic. I met two old men who had worked for the British before 1948. Otherwise it is in people's (largely unhappy) memories that the Mandate is forever burned.

* * *

---

(1) Bentwich, p 75.

Khalil introduces me to my new home. The apartment is large and airy, on the fifth floor of a six-storey building. It is in the very centre of town in an expensive yet nondescript, modern building. My neighbours are middle class Palestinian families. If the number of children I see on the stairs is a guide the families are large. Khalil later told me that the university used this flat and all its other off-campus property as classrooms so that teaching could continue when the Israelis closed down the Palestinian universities during the intifada. I feel extravagantly looked-after in the context of my surroundings. One set of windows opens on to a busy street that leads to the open-air vegetable market. Other windows look out over a partly worked-on and apparently abandoned Roman archaeological site (the hippodrome, most likely), blocks of low-rise flats with washing hanging from their windows and a street lined with taxi ranks, until the land starts to rise sharply up the slopes of Mt Ebal. The mountain looms over the town. It fills my kitchen window so that for a few weeks I always started my breakfast in a state of mild disorientation, as if my mind was searching for an horizon or roofline to judge other angles by. Ebal's lower reaches are covered by urban development, which become less planned and connected about a third of the way up the slope, isolated houses quickly giving way to mountain scrub.

I begin to pick up a sense of the person – a woman – who lived in the flat before me. There are English language books, tapes of Arab and western music and various mementoes, hairpins and a comb in the cupboards, three small airline-style bottles of spirits and many large ones of mineral water, and two large pitta-style loaves wrapped in plastic in the fridge. A small table is covered with containers of white sugar, tea and coffee ready for use. She - or they – has left something of her presence here.

The next morning Khalil gave me a proper introduction to the people on his floor of the main university building. This seems familiar territory to me – academic, western-oriented university life. Is it the same everywhere in the world? An Najah is the largest Palestinian university and the only one funded mainly by the government. Like the other seven, it was formed in the years of amazing educational fervour that followed the Israeli occupation in 1967, when Palestinians hoped that learning would put right the injustices they suffered. Its campus, already badly overcrowded, is almost new, the white stonewalls and arches reflecting the bright light. It looks out from the lower slopes of Mt Gerizim over the once-Christian district of Rafidia. Everything else in my unfamiliar new universe seems to possess a depth of experience I cannot identify. Layers of meaning are struggling for expression. After the introductions I went into the town and a restaurant in Nablus' main square for a late lunch – my first foray into local life. The young waiter spoke very serviceable English. It is going to be difficult to escape being seen as a tourist unless I learn more Arabic.

A wonderful practice is followed on my floor of the main university building (I don't know if it extends further than that): Daoud, the porter, brings Khalil and me a small Arab coffee (strong, with cardamoms) or a glass of tea in our office every few hours, or on request. He always does this with a smile and a word of greeting. He is small and he bends forward a little, giving an impression of being frail; his eyes are both alert and tired and his straggly moustache underlines the slackness of his caring face. He has a marvellously alive and happy demeanour, often giggling uncontrollably. He is a sheikh in his local mosque[1] and his home is high up in the wall of the Old City. After a week or two he told me he earns only 20 shekels (£4-25p) for 9½ hours a day. This is very little on which to bring up his two (or three) children, even in the context of what is a low cost of living by European standards. He wondered if I would give him a reference for another job. I felt pulled between his wishes and what I picked up would be the disapproval of the university authorities if I did this. As it happens, I think he has a good chance of getting a job in the town hall of the local council (baladiyya). To set against official disapproval however, I must set Daoud's kindnesses. Later, when I was down with 'flu, he walked the 250 yards each day to my apartment with a large container of soup and, when we met during street celebrations, he insisted on buying me cake that cost a significant fraction of his day's earnings.

✳ ✳ ✳

---

(1) There used to be three kinds of sheikh. Two were and still are religious – an official in the mosque and a religious leader. The third kind was a landowner in Bedouin society, a man of high standing in local communities. The latter rank has now all but disappeared.

The town is beginning to reveal itself. An abiding impression is of its makeshift nature. Buildings seem to have been thrown up without regard to beauty or permanence since the 1927 earthquake. This gives rise to a tremendous sense of bustle and energy and of living in the present. And yet the town *is* beautiful. Once they leave the central area, streets either rise up the mountain slopes or follow a northwest-southeast axis, so that a backward glance reveals the two mountains rising out of the surrounding farmland. From almost any point stupendous views appear in the sharp bright light – across a valley clustered with fig trees and olive groves, along a slope of houses and gardens that disappears into still azure sky, through criss-crossing urban streets to shimmering mauve rock and scrub.

I quickly found my way to the souks – and almost as quickly was lost in the labyrinth. I asked for directions from a dignified looking man who had just come out of a nearby shop. He said he owned the shop, which was on the ground floor of what was once the Ottoman and British Governors' residence and at some point was used as a prison for women. He is a graduate in engineering of the American University of Istanbul but had been forced to take up this small-scale commercial activity; he said most graduates are similarly under-employed on the West Bank. He believed the effect of the intifada was bad – economically it drained precious resources and socially it gave young people the feeling they need not study hard because their experience as fighters gave them great prestige. As if to emphasise his point he told off two young boys who suddenly ran across our path. He said 'education is the chief asset of a people', or words to that effect.

Khalil said that Nablus and the West Bank had no police force from 1948 until very recently (Jordan and Israel presumably fearing their potential as trained insurgents). About 100 Palestinian policemen have just arrived, trained I think in Jericho, where the Palestinians have partial autonomy. Very young men (they seem about 18-20 years old), they are unarmed and are confined to traffic duty. They try valiantly to cope with the seemingly untameable driving habits displayed at a couple of particularly bad intersections in the city centre. There are no traffic lights, which was explained as a response of the Israeli military to fears of their jeeps being attacked in a traffic build-up. Thus Khalil explained the frequent use of the horn and the general congestion on the roads. And I had assumed, possibly from watching old Hollywood films, that the centres of old Arab towns were terrorised by impatient drivers hooting at pedestrians and at hucksters on mule-back! No one bothers to use belts in cars, even though Israeli regulations require it. I've yet to discover if the risk of being fined in an Israeli court merely reflects a devil-may-care attitude to driving or if it is defiance of the Israeli authorities and a subtle form of patriotism. There are few paved walkways outside the centre so pedestrians must use the sandy strips that often separate roads from shops and building sites. The sounds and sights of a cross-town walk (for this British town dweller) make for a cacophonous and highly social experience. On my first Muslim Holy Day I was surprised to find my favourite restaurant and a number of city centre and local shops open. Having read of the substantial Orthodox following in the town I expected a stricter observance of the Holy Day.

What are my early impressions? Street life is sociable and relaxed; lots of children play in the central residential areas. People seem proud, earnest and friendly. Yet, I sense something subdued in people's behaviour. Political discussion is mostly in the abstract or is reverential of Palestinian leaders. Conversation suggests there is little experience of *participation* in politics. Students often ask me, soon after we are introduced, how I perceive the West Bank (and sometimes, the university). A comparison is implied and I feel that everyone wants to hear that the country measures up to international standards, because the questioners have no yardstick to judge themselves against. Still further behind the question lies a bruised pride that desperately wants to be validated. To balance the weight of indignity and acutely limited rights and opportunities and to sustain personal and national honour my questioners have only the (receding) memory that the Palestinians built most of the economies and social services of the Gulf States in the 1970s and 1980s with their engineers, scientists, managers, lawyers, doctors and craftsmen, and that they have one of the highest university graduation rates in the world. Little do these achievements seem to ameliorate economic conditions or reward national aspirations at this moment.

Except for those on business or in the professions almost all men wear jeans, and sweatshirts under leather jackets. A few wear the kaffiyeh (headscarf) and occasionally one sees an older man in a gallabiyya (loose white cotton gown). A majority of women wear the hijab (headscarf) and dresses that reveal only the hands. I only remember seeing older women wearing skirts in Ramallah, a somewhat less Orthodox town with a large Christian population. Occasionally a man rides or pulls a donkey through the streets; the camels that H V Morton noticed on his urban walks 60 years ago are gone.[1] Only very occasionally does English supplement Arabic on placards advertising professional services and businesses. Signs of a recent stimulation of inner-city commerce and suburban residential development catch the eye. The brash facades of some of the new branch banks shout at you; seven have been built in the last 16 months. Yet there is something missing: industry is small-scale and rudimentary. Almost everything in the shops comes from Israel or abroad. Israeli restrictions on industrial growth are exhaustingly Byzantine, a local businessman told me: few projects get past the Israeli planners' scrutiny.

I'm surprised to find features of life that replicate those in Britain. For example, the generation gap between the shopkeeper in the souk and the lively young boys he told off; murmurings of professional pride and rivalry I picked up in the university; the international 'culture' of TV football and Coca-Cola drinks. I feel somehow cheated. Shops are full of made-in-Israel tinned fruit in a land replete with oranges, guava and other fruits. The restaurants I've visited contain anonymous or international styles of furniture. Even the ability of many young men to reply in good English to my beginner's Arabic seems to mock my search for an 'authentic' Arab culture. Clearly, these cultural manifestations reveal little about the deeper character of the West Bank and I haven't visited many people in their homes yet. I must stay alive to what is happening. Yet, having said all that, there is the reverberating voice of the muessin calling the faithful to prayer, the cacophony of traffic noises, the sharpness of the light, the white dust that settles everywhere, the magnificent over-arching presence of the two mountains above the town; all these are poignantly special. And the centrality of the family in people's lives has a great attraction for me. I'm often asked on first acquaintance if I have children and if they are married.

---

(1) H V Morton, *In the Footsteps of the Master* (1934; London, 1984) p 158.

Ultimately though it is the spirit and resilience in the face of adversity that offers me a key to the Palestinian people I've met so far. For this is not a free or prosperous land. I could easily romanticise the exotic features here and forget this numbing fact. I am nonetheless left wondering how deep is change and what is the effect of Israeli control? Will the western version of modernisation triumph ultimately? Or will it incorporate Islamic and Arab mores? Someone said to me (Rishou maybe): 'We must be the most famous (or discussed or known) people in the world' with obvious pride, wanting me to confirm or share his feelings.

Everyone seems to be up and about by 5:30 in the morning. Children are shouting and car horns blaring in the street below, which is already bathed in strong sunlight. I told a student friend from a nearby village that I am woken by the sound of donkeys braying, followed by the barking of dogs about 5:00 every morning. He said this was true in his village too, except that these noises were preceded by the honking noise made by frogs about 4:30. I generally end my day about 11:00. It feels a short night. I go to bed at an English hour and wake at a Palestinian one. This is infinitely better than the nights spent by the citizens of nearby Tulkarm, however. Packs of dogs are reported to rampage through the streets every night, barking incessantly. Everyone locks themselves behind their doors from 11:00 at night. No one knows why the dogs come or where they go in the daytime.

In the evening the town turns inward; virtually everywhere closes by 6:00. Only a restaurant or two or a corner shop tempt me from the flat. I've heard vague mention of a cinema facility but no one has an address. The absence of evening fare such as cinemas, theatres and cafes is understandable in view of the recently imposed curfews and the social introversion the people have become used to since the intifada. Orthodox Islam frowns on aspects of social behaviour that play a large part in western life, like taking alcohol, and this might also be a factor in Nablus. But the extra deprivation I experience is the absence of that particular kind of semi-privacy that you can enjoy in the daytime in a Western café. The daytime cafes here are filled with men in close conversation; conviviality is an Arab joy, and a solitary stranger stands out like a piece of grit in an oyster. In this intimate town foreignness attracts constant attention. I'm surprised by how much reliance there is on television, especially satellite, for entertainment and keeping up with political developments in the region. There is little else to do in the camps anyway, but the town seems to succumb in sympathy. This makes me think of Britain during the Blackout.

I have solved the mystery of the woman who occupied my flat. Her name is Rose; she is European and teaches here. Like many others, including myself, she often stops for a chat in the office of Ayya, a light-hearted and considerate secretary, who has a wonderful way with people who are a little lost and want a shoulder to lean on.

Two indirect, personal associations with the Arab world keep coming to mind. Pictures I've seen of British soldiers in Palestine under the Mandate evoke memories of my father, who fought in the Great War. It has something to do with the similarity of the uniform. Moreover, Arabic words like *bint, shufti* and *backsheesh* (corrupted into buckshee), were familiar in the slang of my youth in the 1950s, not to mention more established words like mufti and khaki. Partridge's *Dictionary of Slang and Unconventional English* (1951 and 1961 editions) has them all. They derive from use by army or RAF servicemen in the Near East between 1880 and the end of World War Two, though buckshee was taken up in the 18th Century. When I mention them to friends of my age they remember them with some surprise; I never hear them in England now. However, my 1998 computer spell check recognises all five Arabic words in English except backsheesh, and even then it accepts buckshee. They may have disappeared from the lexicon of my friends but they seem to be holding on somewhere in the English-speaking world.

Soon after I'd settled into my flat Khalil replied to my query about my being mistaken for an Israeli if I ventured beyond the city limits: 'No. You are too fair. Also, people can tell the difference. In any case, the Israelis are too afraid to appear here without guns in their hands.'

Two students invited me to a gathering in the university where the death of a leader of Islamic Jihad, who was assassinated in London a few days before, will be mourned. Israel has refused to allow his body to be brought back. I stopped for a while. The main precinct was filled with maybe 250 students. They stood in dignified silence while a small band of men, some in Orthodox garb, declaimed in dirge-like tones from a stage. The atmosphere was extremely heavy. Direct action against Israel by Islamic militants is quite recent. Islamic Jihad was active from the beginning of the intifada in December 1987. But the Orthodox Islamic leadership was circumspect about the value of fighting in the streets back in the early days of the uprising. Sheikh Yassin, its Palestinian leader, eventually took the decision to create a new fundamentalist underground in 1988; Hamas took its name from the acronym for 'Islamic Resistance Movement.' At first the Israelis authorities gave it support, thinking that religious organisations were a less serious threat to Israeli control than were political ones like the PLO. They also hoped Hamas would undermine the PLO. It was six months before Israel changed its policy and descended on Hamas in the first of a long series of raids. But, as a mass movement working towards the destruction of Israel and the removal of secularism from the West Bank and Gaza (and creation of social service provision that in many localities the PLO cannot rival), Hamas had already put down deep roots.

A few mornings later sounds of chanting and banging of feet on the floor erupted outside my office. The corridor is full of female students demonstrating against the way the administration deals with Islamic students. As strict Muslims the men and women keep apart. The men are presumably congregating on the floor above, where the President has his office. Khalil says the administration will not deal directly with representatives of the Islamic students and has not paid their fees. The students are also demanding better study facilities. Khalil says that this protest and a similar one a few weeks ago are the first such signs of unrest; previously demonstrations only occurred against the Israelis! I happened to mention this later to John, a European Election Observer who has recently arrived and now shares the flat with me, and he was surprised, reminding me that the townspeople and students of Nablus have always had a reputation for being 'bolshie'.

The withdrawal of the Israeli army from Nablus is being celebrated with effusions of joy. There has been three days of bustling and loud public holiday. The streets are full of smiling people, car hooters sound even more insistent than usual, and balconies and car windows are festooned with flags and streamers. No one bothers about the explosions. In fact, a fireworks display I came across

Nablus. Dancing in the streets after the Israeli withdrawal.

in Al Hussain Square yesterday teatime seemed moderate and predictable by comparison. The new Palestinian police are the centre of attention as they mingle with the crowds. About 1,200 in all will soon arrive. They are treated with awe and they enjoy the attention. They are armed and wear red, green or black berets, or none, and seem to be drawn from many separate units. Many of them walk around smoking. Order has been imposed on road traffic now that there is a policeman at every road intersection. Snarl-ups seemed interminable before, but they may be a thing of the past.

The new police are quickly establishing the legitimacy of the Palestinian National Authority. They have made a number of raids to collect unlicensed arms. One sweep brought in 22 members of an armed group calling themselves 'Fatah Hawks' who are accused of killing and wounding collaborators. They were active against the Israelis during the intifada and their leader was arrested many times. They resurfaced in Nablus a few months ago. Defiance of the Israeli army is almost certainly a motive behind the explosions in the last few weeks. However, it's more likely that the loud ones I heard at

Fari'a camp yesterday were celebratory. Today, my taxi negotiated separate Palestinian and Israeli checkpoints outside Nablus. I have a strong feeling that the Israeli cordon around the town has been tightened and, after the euphoria has died down, a more measured sense of the reality of 'independence' will appear. There has been an armed guard at the entrance to my block of flats for the last few days. John explained that the regional headquarters of the Palestinian Security Service has been set up on the floor below us.

* * *

I've taken to eating in a restaurant run by Mahmoud. He manages it, sometimes with the help of a brother, for his father. As I got to know Mahmoud, I fell into the habit of eating there shortly before it closes so that he and I can stay talking over a cold drink into the evening. Sometimes we are then joined by one of Mahmoud's family or friends or the dentist with an office on the floor above. The conversation usually takes in the peace process and Palestinian and Israeli politics, but I've learned a lot listening to Mahmoud on Palestinian culture. He has a wide circle of friends and sometimes ropes them in when his good but rusty English fails him. Mahmoud is about 30; his fiancee lives in Jordan. He manages the business with easy authority, and with flair that is the more impressive because it is under-played. He commands the area by the pay desk and the door like an affable major-domo, his cap at a jaunty angle, giving sparse instructions in a quiet voice that carries surprisingly far. His last job of the day is to give the workers their wages and he sometimes looks tired by then. A job he keeps for himself is to transfer the basting chickens from the oven in to a large receptacle; this operation takes place near the doorway within a foot of passing shoppers. There could be dangerous consequences if the hot fat dripping from the birds were to fall on someone. The chickens, whole and halved, are placed next to the large vats of other food from which the waiters can assemble the two or three staple meals in the restaurant. The vats contain pickles (gherkins, cucumbers, chillies, peppers and red cabbage), spiced and finely chopped salad, balls of fried, mashed chickpeas with herbs (falafal), hummus in olive oil, and piles of large pitta-style bread. When I first ordered chicken and salad, expecting the size of portions one might get in Britain, I was horrified to have put in front of me a whole chicken on one plate and a huge pile of marinated vegetables on another plate, with two large pitta-style breads alongside.

We have taken to driving around the town, already dark by closing time. I have now, for the first time, seen the town at night from high up Mt Ebal, the lights sparkling below in the way that waves pick up the light from a passing ship. An Israeli military listening post sits on the summit, preventing us going any further. On another day we passed the only source of liquor in Nablus, the concessionaire apparently being an erstwhile collaborator. Vague figures of men hurried between the door and their cars. Mahmoud said that some prominent men of the town buy drink here. One evening we visited the shop on the outskirts of town that belongs to a relative. As we left, Mahmoud pointed out a small group of men whose body language gave a threatening no-nonsense message as they lounged by their cars. He said, 'They are naughty men – they all have guns in their pockets.'

He told me he had spent two years in an Israeli gaol. He felt no rancour however and recalled the good times before the intifada when Israeli and other tourists and many local people came to the restaurant. He could earn 4,000 shekels a day compared to 10 or so during the Uprising. And, he reminisces, people were then more friendly and polite to each other. There was negligible crime and addiction abuse. He believed the intifada caused more bad than good. By opening their job market to Palestinians again, when the intifada subsided a few years ago, the Israelis were trying to head off further resistance. Things are improving as a result. Today, he said, workers with permits to cross into Israel earn 100-200 shekels a day compared to the 40 shekels received by those on top pay in his own restaurant. Mahmoud is optimistic about his people's future material wellbeing but is filled with foreboding about almost everything else. He is sure the Israelis will not loosen their grip and foresees another Uprising within 15 years. Even though he loves the West Bank and Nablus, he hopes, for the sake of the children he looks forward to having, to leave, probably for the USA. He bleakly reminded me that the Koran tells of the peoples in this region enduring a history of blood, and it has been so for 2,000 years. He was saddened by the fact that local people were now quite callous about injuries and imprisonment suffered during the Uprising. When he was younger he would have helped anyone who was shot or detained; in those days everyone was looked after and the rich helped the poor. Now, so many are injured or have lost a relative or been humiliated that he feels unable to offer much sympathy to sufferers. His younger brother Maher is very angry about what he perceives as the absence of democracy in the forthcoming election. "'Chairman' Arafat will allow no opposition,' he asserted to me in his boisterous manner. At the same time Maher is dismayed by the West's view of Arabs as terrorists, sex-mad and still riding on camels.

Thinking of Mahmoud's family brings a fact to mind: many more refugees in the West Bank live in towns and villages than in the camps. Mahmoud's situation gives the impression of bourgeois contentment. Yet, his parents fled from Jaffa to Amman in 1948. They only returned to the West Bank a few years ago. Unlike Mahmoud, his father would still prefer to return to the land his family left in what is now Israel. His father's life is certainly a success story. He entered the provision trade before taking over their present restaurant and now has interests abroad too. Personal observation tells me that his economic resilience is not typical of city refugees, however. Money for commercial development is difficult to come by, spending power is low and the growth of local industry is hindered by Israeli controls.

The question of hospitality has begun to preoccupy me. How far can I adapt to local culture without offending my own social susceptibilities? I stopped going to Mahmoud's restaurant for a while because he would never accept when I offered to pay for meals. When he said something to the effect that my job as a lecturer entitles me to special treatment I was puzzled. Now a similar issue has arisen with another friend, Walid. After deferring to his strongly expressed desire to pay every time (although with reservations latterly), I could not restrain the effects of my western social training (is it individualism?) and finally insisted on paying one day in the university refectory. Walid became extremely angry, said burst out, 'You mustn't do this!' and promptly paid the bill. Occasionally I have insisted on paying when Khalil and I eat together; he seems to accept my need, presumably because he admires and is very attentive to western practices. But perhaps he also feels less need to assert local practices before a foreign guest who is financially comfortable. I am extremely respectful of social customs and make every effort to accommodate them. A strong feeling of being treated like a child arises when this happens, as my dignity or pride asserts itself. But I am continuing to bite my tongue on these occasions because I want to live as true as I can to Palestinian customs. Nonetheless, my head occasionally echoes with a fierce internal argument before diplomacy finally wins.

* * *

At first 4 November seemed like any other day, but this soon changed. My plans to meet my family in Haifa went badly astray. They were coming on a ship, courtesy of one of my daughters who was an officer on board. But I had no authorisation to get past the armed guard at the dock and had to leave empty handed. I was in some turmoil. Even then, I was able to rescue something from the day. I called at Khalil's home, which is on the taxi route south from Nazareth, had a lovely meal with the family and was able to mention some of my feelings, before going back to Nablus with them by car.

I didn't then realise (not having access to English papers or my new little radio for BBC World Service) that Yitzhak Rabin was assassinated in Tel Aviv while I was sitting with Khalil's family. I was too engrossed in my own feelings to think about the relativity of private and public pain. This seems to have thrown the peace process wide open and revealed the raw contradictions that lie at the heart of Israeli society. In any case, although there is respect for Rabin in the West Bank, there is no love, for he has a considerable reputation as a man of violence.

Rabin fitted into a familiar public niche in Israel as a soldier-turned-senior politician. Because of Israel's peculiar security situation the military have played a greater role at the top of civilian affairs than is usual in the West. Field commanders occupy key posts in the negotiations with the Palestinians and Generals like Dayan, Sharon, Rabin himself (and Barak in 1999) have become leading government ministers. Rabin was a career soldier into early middle age and was Commander in Chief in the Seven Day War of 1967. He retired from the army a year later and spent the next six years as ambassador to Washington. In 1974 he was catapulted straight into the office of Prime Minister during a crisis in the ruling Labour Party. As Minister of War in 1984 he played a major part in the decisions to withdraw from Lebanon and to bomb the PLO headquarters in Tunis. Thus far he may be said to have followed a military career with distinction. Yet, his part as a commando leader in carrying out Ben-Gurion's orders to expel 50,000 Palestinian civilians at gun point from Lydda and Ramleh in 1948 casts another light on his view of military conduct. Nonetheless, unlike many others who have not questioned their own certainties, he was able to face unpalatable options. He walked his 'Road to Damascus' during the intifada. Thrown off-balance by the scale and persistence of this popular uprising his first reaction to stone throwing by youths was to allow the troops to use live ammunition, before he instituted a policy of 'force, might and beatings', including the use of batons, after international criticism had reached a crescendo. 615 (mostly civilian) Palestinians died in two years under this policy. He was impatient with the due process of law when dealing with the revolt and had to be reined in by the Israeli courts on a number of occasions. He first put forward peace proposals in 1989 but the opportunity to explore them only came when he was again Prime Minister in 1992. The Scud attacks during the Gulf War raised questions over the value of keeping the West Bank as a security asset. Realising that armed soldiers could not put down a truly popular uprising, Rabin agreed to talks with the PLO, the outcome of which was the Oslo Accords of 1993. The earlier policy had achieved little except many dead on both sides. In the context of Israeli politics he was seen as a moderate when compared with Begin, Shamir, Sharon (and later, Netanyahu). However, under his government, settlements in the West Bank and Gaza were expanded as rapidly as under right-wing Likud governments. Yet he questioned his own, long-held policies, thought the impossible thought, and negotiated with the Palestinians when many of his fellow countrymen were prepared to stay in denial. He realised not only that he could not defeat the Palestinians but also that Israeli society might fall apart over the issue of territorial expansion. In the end he showed he had vision and courage and was touched with greatness.

What will happen to the peace process now, not only between Israel and the Palestinians, but also between Israel and the Syrians over the Golan Heights, taken by Israel in 1967 at the same time she overran the West Bank and Gaza? Rabin was in the process of negotiating 'land for peace' – giving back land captured in 1967 for a guarantee against attack from her two most implacable enemies, Syria and the Palestinians (with the rider that Syria would also rein in the Shi'ite Hizbulla fighters in southern Lebanon). Rabin had come close to a framework deal with Syria. But the anti-peace party is strong and loud in Israel; it lost the last election by a small margin. Rabin's death offers them the chance to regroup.

The Palestinian anti-peace forces are hovering in the wings too. We are in unknown territory.

* * *

A night visit with Mahmoud to the edge of the Samaritan shrine on Gerizim drew my mind to the congested history of that mountain. The Samaritans are a direct link with the Biblical past. They are a dissident Jewish sect which recognises only the first five books of Moses as inspired scripture. Jews of an Orthodox persuasion refuse to recognise them. Their Holy Place is this mountain and they believe it is older than the Garden of Eden and that dust from it was used in the creation of Adam. They are adamant that its peak remained above the Flood and that it was the site of the original Jewish Temple. They claim that Solomon built the Temple in Jerusalem for personal, not religious reasons. They also believe the rock where Abraham was prepared to sacrifice his son Isaac was on Gerizim, not at the Temple Mount in Jerusalem. They sacrifice seven lambs at Passover on the mountain summit. A Samaritan priest recently gave an account of their history, which emphasises the place of Gerizim in Jewish dynastic struggles. 'We left Egypt...under the leadership of Moses. There were 12 tribes. After we entered the Holy Land we remained one community until Solomon passed away. Later divisions started to take place among Samaritans. People started to complain about the heavy taxes collected by Solomon for building the Temple [in Jerusalem] that contravened the original Temple built on Mt Jarzim (sic) overlooking Nablus. The Tabernacle, known as the tent of the meeting, was made by Moses in Sinai, and transferred to Mt Jarzim by Joshua ben Noun (the same Joshua who destroyed Jericho). At that time, our people refused to submit [to the rule of Solomon's son] and replaced him with another called Yarba'am. From this point onward we called ourselves "Shayrim", which means "Conservatives". The word was developed and the people became known as Samaritans'.[1] This account does not dispel the controversy that shrouds their origins. A major reason for the split between Israeli tribes in the north (Samaria) and south (Judea) seems to have been the refusal of the northern tribes to accept the dynastic aspirations of the family of the southern ruler, David. After the Assyrians defeated the northern tribes in 722 BC, thousands were

---

(1) *Jerusalem Times*, 5 January 1996.

resettled in Mesopotamia and other peoples were transferred to Samaria to replace them, which some believe led to a dilution of the faith. One view has it that they are descendents of the people of five towns who had been deported to Palestina where they 'worshipped Jahweh but served their own gods.'[1] Jesus seems to be referring to them when he spoke to the Woman at the Well of those who 'worship what [they] do not know.' (John: 4.2). Whatever their relation to the Jewish faith the Samaritans seem once to have been a numerous people who suffered savage depredations. Not long after Jesus met the Woman at the Well Pontius Pilate sent troops to massacre those who gathered near Gerizim expecting to be shown sacred vessels left there by Moses. About 30 years later, in the early stages of the Jewish Revolt, a huge gathering of Samaritans took place on their holy mountain. In excess of 11,000 were killed by Emperor Vespasian's soldiers. A series of revolts followed. Some sources claim that 100,000 were massacred when the Emperor Justinian put down their revolt in 529AD. The arrival of the Arabs in the 7th century continued this story of decline: many converted to Islam and the remainder preserved their identity by keeping a low profile. Only in the 18th century were they able to buy land on their holy mountain and resume their holy rites there. Their numbers are small today, some 300-400 in Nablus and in a smaller settlement in Holon, Israel. In modern times most Nablus Samaritans have been relatively poor retailers or artisans, a few being scribes or accountants to the rich of the town.

Outside the town centre my walks generally take me in one of two directions – southwest through the souks and the old City and northwest to Rafidia. The latter district, which extends from the lower slopes of Mt Gerizim almost into the centre of town, holds a particular attraction. It retains something of its origins as a Christian village, although a walk along the main suburban artery reveals only an above-average number of shops and two of the four restaurants in Nablus I've located so far. However, behind the main street lies a Catholic school; small, stone-built, it has a sturdy Ottoman look. When a friend and I sat outside one of its windows one hot mid-afternoon, tired after a walk in the nearby countryside, a sister greeted us almost immediately with a few words, a jug of water and some biscuits. A short distance away, just before the

---

(1) Servotte, *According to John*, p24.

land shelves down to a valley, many small, intricately laid-out gardens cling to the crest. Something about them looks old – the fine, dark tilth of the soil that only years of labour could create, their child-like scale, the designation of boundaries of the slim strips by occasional bushes and decorated poles? Vegetables and herbs have been lovingly tended and have responded luxuriantly in what would otherwise be a dry and arid soil on these high slopes. A few, tumbledown stone houses stand nearby, clustered around a courtyard. I imagine an obscure inheritance document lying in a vault somewhere that prevents the modernity of Nablus from sweeping them aside.

Their worn stone doors and windows, occasionally decorated and inscribed, say that they are obstinately of another age. Presumably this area belonged to the farmers of the old village, when it was independent of Nablus. The courtyard was probably intended to contain livestock, though only chickens and a goat forage there as I watch. The intimacy of this arrangement is endearingly different – an affront to the modern penchant for privacy. The present families look out of their kitchens straight in to their neighbours'. This openness to neighbourly curiosity (so reminiscent of life in the camps and in the Old City wall!) contrasts starkly with the isolation of the flat-dwellers in the blocks that have spread up the hill from Nablus. I wonder how many of Rafidia's inhabitants share my feelings for this enclave.

Some of the differences between the West Bank and Britain are striking. There is a great dearth of public capital here. The (private) Palestine Research Centre in the town is well equipped, perhaps better than comparable departments in An Najah, yet (I am told) it does not work hand-in-hand with the university. In addition, environmentalism is having a very hard struggle. The streets are congested with the invariable (and often old) Mercedes cars and taxis. The old buses belch fumes. There are no means of saving glass and cans and the big refuse containers in the city centre are few, usually overflowing and the home or larder to many cats. I thought the vegetable market I frequent had excellent 'green' credentials. The produce comes fresh every morning from local farms and the vegetables are some of the largest I've seen. Remembering the controversy in Britain over the use of chemicals on crops I mentioned the market to one of the European Observers (who have appeared in town to monitor the imminent, first national elections). He swept away my romantic notions by pointing out that a lack of local controls means that farmers are free to douse the vegetables with DDT, which has been banned throughout most of the West, although it is still being peddled in the third world by western manufacturers. Finally, young people are desperate for work and decent economic and social opportunities. Almost half the population is below 15 years of age. So many young men want to leave the West Bank! For example, Khalil's son and the young worker in Mahmoud's restaurant, who told me, 'There is nothing here.' Mahmoud agreed that the young want to leave. I realise all these features owe something to a lack of representative government and the effect is to limit people's life chances.

An English friend has arrived for a short visit. We went to Assyra al-Shamaliya, a village on the other side of Mt Ebal from Nablus, which was recommended for its tranquil atmosphere. It is an old farming village serving Nablus market, yet it has all the qualities of an Elysian dream. The nearby houses cluster around the mosque; a few steps away large gardens and fields begin to intermingle with outlying farmhouses as the land falls away to olive groves. Other hill villages hover on the horizon. Standing briefly outside one house to admire the view we were immediately invited in by the farmer and his family. His wife immediately destroyed my image of the deferential and submissive Arab wife. She let here husband lead the conversation in the remnants of the English he acquired as a young man during the Mandate. But he, a gentle person who also looked rather ill, seemed totally happy to let his wife, in her warm and enclosing way, provide a secondary source of interaction, as she talked to us almost non-stop in Arabic when she was in the room and sometimes interrupted him with a remark and a burst of laughter. She and her daughters ate with us, a deviation from Arab custom. The moment we left this easy conviviality, three men who were bringing goats and donkeys from the fields offered us hospitality and we were soon sitting amongst olive trees in their family garden sharing cakes and tea. One young man taught me how to handle one of the small wooden ploughs behind a donkey. I've watched this operation from afar many times on the journey to Jerusalem. An insurance man on his rounds appeared through an olive grove at one point. Before he disappeared into the trees again in the opposite direction he talked quickly and passionately in English about life under occupation.

CHAPTER 4

Khalil

So much depends on Khalil's judgement and contacts. How will we take to each other?

MY FIRST IMPRESSION is of a slight, dapper and self-contained man. Now I see he is fired by personal and national ambition. He has a small moustache, sparkling bespectacled eyes and an infectious chuckle. He sees something humorous in most things, yet he carries a strong sense of responsibility for his family, job and people. His business-like manner and economy of effort are reflected in an admirably uncluttered desk. His clan is a major landowner to the north of here, where historically it was responsible for the welfare of the peasants. As the near-feudal ties in the Palestinian countryside began to dissolve earlier this century, big families like his began to educate their sons into the professions. Khalil gives the impression of being very at ease in society.

I enjoyed many revealing discussions in his company. One example was a dinner at his house. I travelled there with two other guests. Benny is Jewish; serious and outspoken, he vehemently opposes his country's occupation of the West Bank and Gaza. His gravitas has an attractive quality, especially when his eyes are softened by the occasional twinkle. He greeted our fears that the car he was driving might not complete the journey, because of the way it sways along on its collapsed suspension, with a robust jokiness that brooked no contradiction. Abdul, who works in the university administration, is quietly at ease. His informed comments on the political scene are expressed in an easy familiarity with English idiom.

After dinner we inevitably talked of national affairs. Khalil believes that salvation for Palestinians lies in their institutions. Trade unions, religious charities, universities, schools and Non-Government Organisations can mediate between the people and the Authority – if the latter listens to them. It all depends on the openness of the still-young Palestine National Authority to informed opinion and dedicated people. He wrote to the powers-that-be about this some while ago. Khalil has a reassuring presence, expressed in his insights, subtleties and heartfeltness. His ambition is driving him very hard yet his heart warms to his family and his town and he yearns after a settled future for the refugees and the Palestinians. Abdul said that, since the beginning of the intifada, people have largely kept to their homes in the evening and have been exposed to a lot of television. Media image-building and propaganda have played a big part in consolidating power at the top, counteracting the devolution of power to the communities that we associate with the intifada. The Palestinian people know what is happening, he said; they are well educated, but there are no channels through which to voice their views. Everyone agreed the Authority was not accountable or very responsive to the people and that a future Palestine would have some degree of impervious central power after the elections. It is anyone's guess where the future lies, but an opportunity exists for the development of an intriguing blend of democracy and tradition. Here, the mind and heart are always exercised, trying to understand new configurations by reference to the past, and looking hopefully into the future whence we desire to escape the present.

Back in my flat later that evening I went over this discussion again, wondering about the capacity of Palestinian Arab society for change. Aburish[1] argues convincingly that Palestinians have already taken great strides towards modernisation. He also, however, underlines the complexity of this process by pointing to the loyalty of his own village of Bethany near Jerusalem (where Jesus was last seen) to traditional authority and values. The British went some way to respect traditional life. But the Israeli occupation from 1967 was different. The extensive use of collaborators in

---

(1) Said K Aburish, *Children of Bethany* (London, Bloomsbury Press, 1991 edition).

communities and prisons, the creation of puppet leaders (mukhtars) in the Village Leagues (collaborationist bodies set up by Israel to undermine loyalty to clans) and the exposure of young people to drink, drugs and sexual improprieties while working in Israel constituted a direct challenge to social values and to Islam. Thus unsettled, many young men gave their allegiance to the leader of a political faction, which recognised the revolutionary nature of the changes, rather than to a mukhtar or sheikh who was trying to recreate the past. These searching changes could not be predicted. They began only 20 years ago; their working-out will stretch far into the future.

During a break from office routine, while sipping Daoud's coffee, Khalil elaborated on Aburish's views. He believes the clan (or hamula), once the guardian of traditional values and social relations, is in an advanced state of decay. The radical philosophy of the political factions that appeared a decade ago shows little tolerance towards the conservatism and collectivism of the clans. In addition, the imminence of statehood is pushing political discourse on to a different track, one largely determined by the West. Yet, there exist no traditions of democracy that the West recognises. Opinions are not openly thrashed out. It is therefore difficult to achieve a consensus on a future political and social shape of Palestine.

Khalil again echoed Aburish when he mentioned an old custom that lingers in some villages and clans for the leading family to set a house aside where guests can stay. Friends and family of the host contribute food for the guest, not because food is scarce, but as an acknowledgement of the importance attached to hospitality. I seem to have experienced the modern form of this custom. When I'm introduced to someone or visit their home, their friends are also invited round to meet me or I go to their home or workplace. Great pleasure is shown in receiving guests and sharing resources. But I think what I am being treated to is the Arab delight in hospitality, which offers a glimpse of the ceremonial events that villagers once took part in. Mutual support was a feature of the old village system; public land was available for villagers to grow and glean small crops of food and herbs. The poor were assured of a place there. Life now feels more harshly competitive. Khalil said that cultural societies are now appearing, with the intention of making the features of traditional life more widely known to the young. They first appeared in Damascus in the 1980s. One feature of Arab society that has not succumbed to modern influences is the system of family preferment. In what is easy to see with western eyes as nepotism and as an affront to meritocracy, Arab families use family connections to help their children. Rarely are jobs filled by open interviews. Yet, as Khalil says, in a world with little other form of protection, it is to the family you must look for security.

The tug between old and new in the West Bank is probably being played out over a myriad of breakfast tables every day. With a disconsolate expression on his face Khalil admitted that his family wants to enjoy some of the benefits of western life. He said he had virtually given up defending their life under Occupation. He owns a number of landholdings nearby and enjoys walking between two small farms separated by the beautiful slopes of a mountain. His life is fulfilling and balanced. Most of his family do not know the West and find its attractions compelling. Khalil cannot easily understand his family's preferences, yet he laughed at the irony of the fact that he was trained to help others handle the stresses of family life and now that it affects him directly he finds it difficult to practise these skills. This reminds me a little of Bosnian friends in the UK: the children want to stay and their parents feel the tug of their homeland. Here, in the West Bank, the older men in the camps generally want to hold on to old customs and memories of the past whereas younger men are more likely to hunger after material improvements. Khalil said there is a need for a few radical people to challenge academic certainties in the West Bank. His own radicalism and egalitarianism sit comfortably with his love of tradition and formal learning. He is familiar with western approaches and happily shares the table with women. Elsewhere, till now, I've invariably dined only with men and been served by women.

Khalil has a store of regional jokes. I remember a few. One is about Hebronites and is set in a plane that has engine trouble. One Hebronite says to another, 'We will crash. What shall we do?' The other replies, 'Don't worry, this plane isn't ours. We'll not lose anything.' Another is a Jordanian joke (it requires you to know that many Egyptians have settled in Jordan). Four people were travelling in a plane. They were taking things that were plentiful in their country to give to friends. The Egyptian took money, the Syrian took dates, the Palestinian took olives. The plane got into trouble and they were told to ditch anything of which they had too much. The Egyptian threw out some money, the Syrian some dates and the Palestinian some olives. The Jordanian thought for a minute, then he said, 'We have too many Egyptians.' So he threw the Egyptian out of the window. A Palestinian joke recounts that, on the Day of Judgement, everyone began to arrive at the Pearly Gates. But the Palestinians were refused entry. They went to the Gates of Hell and were turned away. So they settled in a refugee camp halfway between Heaven and Hell. A quintessential Palestinian viewpoint on life is expressed by Juha, a wizard or mythical figure who expresses his sharp-eyed wisdom with laconic wit. For example, a neighbour told Juha he had dreamt that the next two years would turn out badly for him. 'What will the years after be like?' he asked. Juha replied, 'You will be OK. You will be used to it by the end of the two years.'

I was given a graphic lesson in the astonishing smallness of this land when Khalil and I attended a conference in Bethlehem. I'd already looked westwards right across the plain of Israel to the town of Netanya on the Mediterranean coast a week before when standing near the West Bank hill village of Jaba'. The mountains of the Jordan Valley were just visible in the opposite direction. It is only a little under 40 miles to Bethlehem. While trying to avoid a military roadblock near Ramallah on the way back, Khalil took a wrong turning. In less than an hour we had driven east to the edge of the Jordan Valley through stunningly beautiful mountains. The high peaks of Jordan were a backcloth to the lower formations this side of the river. The sun played on one or two lower peaks in the foreground while a high darkness raged behind. Back in the flat flashes of lightning and torrential rain dominated the evening. The abnormally-hot autumn weather is beginning to break at last. Khalil promised the rain would last for a week.

The Bethlehem conference was Khalil's metier. Reporters sought his opinion afterwards. The theme was the future of the West Bank and Gaza. The gathering attracted about 15 academics, administrators and politicians. It was conducted in very demonstrative Arabic yet the lectures were punctuated by technical phrases in English. Most people have portable phones, one speaker leaving his on the table, as if in a state of high readiness to leave.

Afterwards Khalil and I visited the Church of the Nativity, where I felt comforted by the simple worn columns, the ornate altar and candelabra and the chanting coming from a small cluster of fathers. The hubbub of the tourists was quiet and respectful as they moved around in a pensive, appreciative way. Nothing jarred. Bethlehem will soon be under Palestinian autonomy for the first time. Soon after the Israeli troops were re-deployed Arafat used the opportunity both to heal some feelings and to wave the nationalist flag by saying, 'Jesus was a Palestinian.'

Israel is in a constant state of readiness for more suicide bombings. There is a reciprocal movement in the violence, to the extent that no one can now identify a moment of beginning. Reaction tends to take place against the latest outburst by 'the other side.' Violence engenders more of the same. I'm becoming convinced however that some of the actions of the Israeli military and security services are a *cause* of Israeli distress. How many Israelis believe this I wonder? It is asking a lot of people to stand up for humanity against their perceived national interest. Yet it strikes me that enlightened self-interest is more likely to be secured by Israel making a big gesture to the Palestinians rather than by using her inordinate military power to maintain a sterile status quo.

The peace process is like a desperately hungry dray horse that keeps stopping when it spies a new piece of grass. Progress is often interrupted by unexplained administrative delays. Now however it has halted while the Israeli election, following Rabin's death, gets underway. Is it really a process towards peace or a continuation of the squeeze on the Palestinians though? And what should the Palestinians do, given their political weakness? The more I talk and think about it the more depressed I feel about the future. I'm convinced that Israel's ability to look beyond short-term military ascendancy is the only hope for the future. An added complication is the war that Israeli society is waging with itself. Perhaps it is the small change that counts. A Druze sergeant was kind to Khalil and me at the Jerusalem checkpoint the other day when we were lost on the way to Bethlehem University. He let us through even though there was some small irregularity in Khalil's documents. Khalil was impressed – one up for the real peace process.

CHAPTER 5

On the Road to Jerusalem

This road is almost impossible. Many people will be killed if something isn't done about its condition and overcrowding.
Remark of a fellow taxi passenger concerning the large number of serious accidents on the northern section of the Nablus-Ramallah-Jerusalem road

THE JOURNEY FROM Nablus to Jerusalem soon took on a familiar shape. Large, seven-seat Mercedes taxis negotiate the 45 miles of tortuous bends in the hills; surfaces are badly pot-holed till we join up with a new road to Israeli settlements near Ramallah. Settlements sit on the top of many hills, their white buildings throwing back the sun, energetic and confident in their newness, muted in their isolation. The few old buses create long queues. As the journey unravels, small topographical details become sharply etched in the memory. Between Nablus and Ramallah, in the narrow upland valleys where fertile land is so scarce, men (and sometimes women and children) ride on or guide donkeys which draw some kind of scratch ploughs (rather like a small cultivator in Britain). As we descend towards Ramallah the valleys broaden out and a few modern tractor-drawn ploughs and larger stretches of ploughland come into sight. Yet, even here, as in the hills, ploughing is usually done in small, regular strips, almost rectangles, suggesting the continuing popularity of donkey power.

The beauty of line and texture of the drystone-walling is stupendous. The walls flow across the rocky hillsides, sometimes filling in the gaps between large boulders, sometimes tracing their own uninterrupted path along what must be the natural declension of the land. The soil, even after ploughing, is so rocky that the soil-to-stone ratio appears to be one-to-one. Presumably this is also the case at greater depths, making stone clearing untenable. Seen from a distance, the tracery of stonewalls and lines of rock, startlingly white where it catches the sun and a soft, animal-underbelly fawn in the shade, perfectly complements the graceful rounded symmetry of the hills themselves. The terraces are divided into small strips or regular patches of highly cultivated, soft brown soil. The soil seemed to lack definition during the mid-winter off-season. Yet a closer look reveals a finely etched pattern of furrows on each terrace. The farmers seem intent on demonstrating how free God has been with his love for this patch of countryside. Ploughing and some cutting back of olive tree growth prepare farms for the sudden up-rush of fertility that is already underway by late-January.

The longer taxi route from Ramallah to Jerusalem takes in a small village with a large tile manufactory at its centre. The main 'road' is acutely dusty and uneven, even by the standards of other towns and villages. We passed small, scattered communities and lean-to, tented family homes (of Bedouin or refugees?) while crossing rocky, broken and open land. Jerusalem's poignantly unresolved skyline of eastern and western oddments was upon us while I was deep in a reverie on this Arab land. White, compact Israeli settlements appeared on my left. In Jerusalem modern Israeli buildings conveyed a message of urgency and assertiveness, even combativeness. My powers of assimilation failed me. The small Arab communities already seemed light years away.

In fact, it is never long before political tensions intrude again. Going south, a little way short of Ramallah, the road climbs a narrow defile in the rock and a minor road feeds in from the right. An Israeli settlement is close by, although just out of sight over the hill. This junction is obviously a site of some importance. It is one of those places where Israelis and Palestinians almost meet. The atmosphere among my fellow passengers seems to be charged, not so much with tension, because the proximity of the peoples here is still arms-length and mutual acknowledgement seems to have assumed the formality of a Japanese No play, but rather with a weary frustration, which causes no discernable rise in emotional temperature. A few armed soldiers stand guard opposite the minor road. A small group of people wait for transport south by Israeli bus or by hitching a lift. They are off-duty soldiers, one man wearing a skullcap, mostly young people. They have come the short distance across the hill from the settlement.

Travelling in a military occupation zone requires me to relish the unexpected. Most taxis rides offered opportunities to talk with my fellow passengers and contemplate the passing scenery. Yet I was shaken by the surreal turn taken by one journey. The taxi left the road and cut through the fields a few miles from Nablus, presumably to avoid the checkpoints half a mile up the road. I realised we were in fact in a line of taxis chasing along the dirt tracks between growing crops. For a while we were in sight of Israeli soldiers. It was rather like taking part in a Keystone Kops car chase. But it was potentially more dangerous of course. Yet, reality seemed to have collapsed for a poignant moment. Then we joined the main road again and things returned to normal. So much for strict security!

Another requirement of travel is adaptability. One day I was a little late catching the Ramallah taxi in Jerusalem. It was only about 5:30 in the afternoon, but somewhere in the back of my mind warning signals were buzzing. When we arrived in the outskirts of Ramallah as dusk set in, among streets that meant nothing to me, the driver said this was the end of the journey. I'd never walked across Ramallah before but was told the way to the centre. On the way I crossed the fruit and vegetable wholesale market, busy in the darkness with men loading crates onto lorries. Asking the way again I was referred to the supervisor in his small hut at the centre of the activity. He told me that no more taxis were running tonight, I forget why, but he offered to let me travel in a lorry delivering vegetables to Nablus in half an hour's time. We struggled to communicate with a mixture of English and Arabic, drinking tea brewed on a small stove kept constantly in use for the workers. Then I travelled in the lorry, which stopped on the way to pick up other stragglers. We slowly made our way, Arab music from the radio just blotting out the growl from a worn exhaust.

Damascus Gate, an entry to the old City in Jerusalem, is the terminus of my journeys. The Gate has many private meanings for me. Here I had my first sight of Palestinians; the Israeli soldier standing above the arch looking down on Muslims crowding through the gate on the way to Friday prayers epitomises the whole sorry conflict; it is the taxi terminus where I go through a metamorphosis from an itinerant researcher in an intensely-Arab Nablus to a life in West Jerusalem where I can at least take some aspects of Israeli westernisation in my stride. It is also the point where I briefly enter Israel, leaving it again at the southeast edge of Jerusalem, having joined in the meantime with some Israeli peace workers on our way to the Beit Sahour peace centre near Bethlehem. I pause for a moment, look around and let the meaning of this place sink in. The process has begun earlier though. My pulse starts running as the taxi negotiates Jerusalem's northern suburbs – then Sheikh Jarrah, St George's Cathedral, the American Consulate, Nablus Road, and we are outside the Gate itself. The feeling of being present to something limitless and sublime has a very physical aspect. The Eternal City draws down a sense of spiritual and physical prostration within moments. And the intensity of street life is palpable. Jerusalem is at the heart of the Israeli-Palestinian imbroglio. The Israelis claim it indivisibly as a Jewish city. The Palestinians claim their capital should be here; it is also the third city in Islam.

On the way to the Beit Sahour peace group for the first time I briefly stopped off to wander in the Old City of Jerusalem. The muted colours seemed translucent as the light changed rapidly during the shortening winter days. The sun went in and a sharp chill began to bite by 2:00. A coffee stop in Ben Yehuda Street brought me sharply back into contact with the West. It is good to be back in Israel and to enjoy familiar things like European coffee and food and a range of English language newspapers. But it is also uncomfortable. I pick up tension in the air – it may account for the abrupt or heated words I've witnessed between people in the street.

At the entry to an old street in West Jerusalem a sign reads: 'Entrance for women dressed immodestly, tourists and groups FORBIDDEN. This is a residence area, not a tourist site. Please don't irritate our feelings!!!' The sign is printed in four languages including Hebrew. The Neighbourhood Council must have been at the end of its tether. There are a number of more serious indications of tension, too. In some central streets about one in four of the men are in army uniform and armed. They generally look young and bored and are inveterate bus travellers, presumably going on and off duty. Occasionally civilians walk around armed with rifles and other large guns. One evening I saw a group of armed vigilantes checking the doors in a side street. On another occasion I was astonished to realise that the man sitting next to a group of children playing in a park near the West Jerusalem YMCA was in fact an armed guard. Walking through the Muslim Quarter in the Old City on two separate occasions I noticed the Star of David sprayed on a door and a wall. There is a heaviness that soon wears me out. Jerusalem Israelis seem to have lost touch with their laughing child. I always feel so relaxed when I enter the West Bank again. Hell! It is so difficult. I've polarised these two peoples. Why do I have to choose? The Israeli Occupation is indefensible and I've been told so much about the indignity and difficulty of life under it. However, I've also noticed some stress and abruptness in the West Bank too. And all of this in the most gregarious peoples I've ever met!

The peace group was an eye-opener. It was conducted in English with about a dozen of us, including maybe four foreigners. I got the group's address from a peace diary; it is obvious its name has spread far. What energy it has! Yet, I wonder how far the people and organisers are willing to shift or challenge their existing positions? Everyone seemed to be operating near the edge of his pain. A rather nervous atmosphere: careful politeness and some laboured jokes. The work of groups like this seems the only way forward at the moment. They have a long road ahead if their mutual memories are to become forces for good and not estrangement.

At the next gathering I spoke with a fellow newcomer. She has only recently left the UK to take up Israeli citizenship. Although in love with the vibrant culture here she is horrified by the rigour of the application process and the response of some people to her belief that Palestinians should be independent. I feel open to the Israeli spirit today. The passion that seems to infuse all human contact here does not exclude a commitment to technical efficiency. Most artefacts are new – buses, things in shops, public telephones, even many houses in the western inner city. Services seem to run to timetable and the variety of consumer choice is vastly greater than that open to Palestinians. And western high culture is abundantly on display. I was particularly in touch with a need for cultural familiarity on this trip. Yet, two unpleasant incidents marred my visit. I'm beginning to think this dark side of life comes as part of the package in Jewish Jerusalem. One was a violent verbal attack by a man on my new friend and me in a Ben Yehuda Street restaurant because we shifted a Hanukkah candleholder a few inches so we could see across the table. We were harangued for not respecting Judaism and the attack continued even when my friend said she was Jewish and Israeli. This may have been because we were speaking in English. The proprietor later said the man was unbalanced, but the memory still stings. The other was an altercation earlier on the Ein Kerem bus between a middle-aged woman and a young man with his feet on a seat. Challenges to unruly behaviour seem to have become a thing of the past in Britain. I was elated by the vigour and social confidence of the woman yet began to sympathise with the youth as he wilted. This is a very diverse and unassimilated society. Religion, culture, country of origin – I knew of these divides, but a generation gap as well! I love the Israeli passion, which is in the air all the time, crackling like static.

My third visit soon became pure theatre. As usual the Jerusalem contingent was picked up by a small hired bus in West Jerusalem to go the short journey to Bethlehem in the West Bank. Beit Sahour is within Greater Bethlehem. On this occasion we were disappointed to see an impromptu security check ahead. An incident must have occurred and, because there were Israelis on board, the bus might be turned back. As we approached the checkpoint a plan was quickly devised by one of the Israeli organisers. We were to pretend to be tourists who could only speak English, on a trip from Jerusalem to Bethlehem; those of us with foreign passports were to sit at the front of the bus and speak to the investigating soldier. Everyone else was to stay silent. As it happened, the soldier chosen to board the bus spoke little English and, looking quickly at a few passports, he soon left and wished us a good journey. The Israelis on the bus made up conversations in English. It was a wonderful performance. I found it difficult to stay with the illusion, wanting to laugh out loud.

The Quakers are a contact point with the peace process. I was looking forward to stopping off on the way to Jerusalem and visiting the local Meeting in Ramallah, which is also one of my few contacts with the western community. Yet the experience of sitting in near-silence for an hour after the gregariousness of my early weeks was a little unnerving. Nonetheless I felt quite a lot better for going to my first Meeting. There were only eight of us there.

I shared a meal afterwards with a foreign scholar who attended the Meeting. He said something about the big families who dominate the town,[1] one family being closely connected to the Quakers, before he suddenly switched tracks in order to broach a matter of personal concern – the price of speaking your mind: 'If you are brave you become lonely here,' he said, without further elaboration. He mentioned the great flexibility of modern Arabic but defined it chiefly as a poetic language, not one that relates well to the tenets of western classical education. He observed that the Koran was written in classical Arabic and not the ordinary language of Mecca, because the language of Mohammed was that used by the upper classes. Modern Arabic has however come into contact with many other languages, such as Persian. That is why, he claimed, most people trained in modern Arabic cannot understand the Koran. Despite this incongruity, the Arabic of the Koran is used as the standard of current cultural discourse. Confusion reigns as a result. Old linguistic misunderstandings combine with modern educational rigidities and political contradictions to stop people debating the meaning of Palestinian cultural identity. The present choice for open-minded Palestinians is either to accept things as they are or to break away, adopt western philosophies, and emigrate. No middle road has been discovered which preserves historical roots while also accepting a selection of what the West is offering. The result, he claimed, is that Palestinians have no distinctive culture – they do not understand their classical origins and yet they resist western culture.

My thoughts strayed back to conversations with Khalil. If Palestinians really misunderstand their classical origins they nonetheless have no doubt about a more immediate issue – the everyday, lived culture of the people. I associate Palestinians with a love of family and nation, with respect for the guiding light of Islam, generosity and hospitality, and gregariousness and sense of brotherhood – as well as extreme pride and touchiness regarding

---

(1) He said there are five; a native of the town mentions seven. Hanan Ashrawi, *This Side of Peace: A Personal Account* (New York, Simon and Schuster, 1995) p 248.

their perceived national character. In any case, which other Arab people has yet come to terms with the almost paralysing sense of loss of the vibrancy, purpose and leadership of the first eight centuries after Mohammed? The ascendancy of the West in modern times is something few Arabs can ignore or fail to lament. Moreover, the situation in the West Bank and Gaza is unique. No other Arab people are under the tutelage of non-Arabs, have greater attainments in higher education or, saving perhaps Lebanon, have a more open democratic system in the making. Although they coexist uneasily, tradition and modernisation have not cancelled each other out. But the situation is also delicate. My fears are more to do with the result of unfettered capitalism sweeping through this land. Will it bolster the autocratic tendencies of the new elite and so widen the existing divisions in society? Are there enough safeguards built into public life for the modern and the traditional to interact fruitfully and flexibly? The answer might indeed be to get back to a bedrock of classical culture, for it strikes me that the people need philosophical and spiritual guidance while they continue to digest the changes of the last 20 years. Capitalism alone offers a fractured, problematic future. There is need of an enduring sense of culture if totalitarianism and repression are to be avoided, if the people are not to be overwhelmed or manipulated.

CHAPTER 6

Refugees at Home: Balata camp

Over half the Palestinian people – refugees displaced by the creation of Israel in 1948 and their descendents – are offered nothing by the [Oslo] accord, but are expected to acquiesce in their own political disappearance and accept resettlement wherever they happen to be.
Najm Jarrah, New Times, 2 October 1993

ZIAD, A UNIVERSITY student who lives in Balata camp, has invited me to eat with his family. Unlike small, rural Fari'a, Balata is a large suburb of Nablus. Balata camp is both awesome and nondescript. I've read and heard so much about it. Two leading Israeli commentators believed it was in the vanguard of opposition to Israeli occupation, even before the intifada erupted in 1987. It became out-of-bounds to Israeli administrators when it closed ranks around a militia of the camps' young men. 'Israeli troops simply preferred to avoid the camp as much as they possibly could.'[1]

Men standing near the entrance look at me searchingly. Ziad's presence reassures them. He has a word of greeting for almost everyone we pass. My first impression is that the camp is small, compact and intense. It is not a shantytown, though the open sewage channels that run alongside the narrow alleyways give that impression initially. Yet the buildings of breeze block are too solid and the main roads too regular for that, and the broken roof-line of water tanks and wires reaching up out of unfinished buildings is typical of much

---

(1) Schiff and Ya'ari, *Intifada*, p 61.

Batala camp alleyway; sewage channel on left.

of Nablus. The families I've visited are fastidiously house-proud in their confined living spaces. The dusty alleys are noticeably free of debris. There is something temporary and something defiantly normal about Balata. Amazingly it is the largest camp on the West Bank, officially containing some 13,000 people, unofficially nearer 18,000. Yet it covers a mere 62.5 acres. Almost twice as many people are crammed into an average home in Balata as in the smaller, distant camp of Fari'a. Alleys and narrow 'streets' separate buildings that stretch upwards after having given up the struggle to take a few more inches from the adjoining roadway. Some houses are only 1' 6"apart: lack of privacy is a byword. The one open space (with a few trees) I saw was the playground of a school. Housing expansion and decay intermix. Using money earned by their sons in Israel or the Gulf in the 70s and 80s perhaps half the householders have remodelled their property in the space available. Many extensions rise above or at the side of the original tiny UNRWA blockhouses, which date from the early 1950s. The inner walls of many of these structures are streaked with mildew, even in the midday heat. The roofs of some have been converted into bedrooms by the addition of rickety corrugated iron roofs, which lean at awkward angles. Some sleeping quarters, even in these confined spaces, are further divided by blankets. The poignant sense of pride conveyed by the well-scrubbed and fading floor tiles in one house made me catch my breath for a moment.

Balata was created from the scattered remnants of many clans drawn from over 60 villages. It contains an unusually larger number of Bedouin from central Palestine, many from the large village of Arab Al-Sawalma. The predominance of Bedouin and the presence of small groups drawn from villages and clans scattered across a large area, along with the very size of the camp, may help to explain the slow build-up of resistance there before the 1980s. These factors militated against the rapid creation of a community spirit, in contrast to the experience of the relatively tiny camp at Fari'a. But when this did occur feelings soon reached flash point. Local factors may also have exacerbated the underlying feelings of resentment. Bad memories survived of the camp's treatment by leaders of Nablus municipality. One mayor said it was better to provide water for donkeys than for Balata residents. Another ordered all camp children out of Nablus schools and dispersed them around surrounding villages.

Although the intifada began to ebb two years ago, there is evidence of it everywhere. Oil drums litter the camp boundary. These were used by troops to block the camp exits. In one alleyway that leads to the Nablus-Ramallah road, presumably a popular escape route, the door to one house was blocked by drums and would only open a few inches. Resistance to the Occupation was apparent as I entered from the direction of town along Jacob's Well road. Graffiti covers the walls nearby, including large drawings of a machine gun and of Al Aqsa Mosque in Jerusalem. 'Fateh (sic) Camp' is written in English on the wall fronting the main street. Camp activists are obviously aware that western journalists sent the name of Balata around the world during the intifada. The words may also illustrate factional rivalry. Support for Fatah, the large mainstream party that dominates the PLO and is led by Arafat, is about 70% compared to 20% for Hamas. Many people, I'm told, still own guns. Although civil disobedience was the chief weapon used against Israeli administrators, and stone-throwing against troops, during most of the intifada, the use of guns became a feature of the conflict from about 1990, at a time when frustration escalated following the killing of 17 Palestinians in the holy Haram al-Sharif precinct on Temple Mount in Jerusalem. Moreover, while gaining very little from the peace process, Palestinians had to watch an influx of Soviet Jews into the occupied territories. A small handgun costs an enormous £1,875 and bullets are 62p each but it is felt that they must have them, so they save every shekel.

Ziad's calm and caring manner is immediately apparent. Although only about 5' 9" he appears taller; he is solidly built with an unexpectedly soft rumbling voice. He lost an eye and has a leg injury after being shot by Israeli soldiers in the Camp two years ago. As he takes me round the camp, at his quiet insistence, he expresses pride in the camp's achievements, especially in the half-finished social centre on the camp's perimeter on Jacob's Well road. His sense of responsibility expresses itself in an unflappable response to daily irritations and disappointments. He is the sort of person I would turn to for impartial advice and so it was no surprise to learn he is now a leader of the main political faction in the camp and is prominent in student politics. His grandfather was a Bedouin sheikh who owned land in what is now coastal Israel. We talked with two of his Balata friends, Hassan, who combines manual work with part-time study at the Palestinian Open University in Jerusalem, and Zakkaria, a dentist. All three young men (around 28-35 years old) have spent time in Israeli gaols. Because of their security record Ziad and Hassan cannot work in Israel.

In the evening we walked to the main street to buy falafal. Men stood around in small clusters; women kept on the move, presumably with a domestic purpose in mind. When it was our turn to be served, the owner of the shop, learning of my nationality, expressed his anger against Britain for encouraging Jews to come to Palestine. As a small crowd gathered this older, white-haired man spoke passionately and yet with acute politeness. He said he once owned land in Israel around Lud and Jaffa (and he of course says he still does) and dreamed always – and for his children – of returning. He was puzzled by the talk of a UN offer of compensation to the refugees because he would be expected to give up his dream. How could anyone expect him to do this? He was warm and friendly towards me, including me in the circle of his friends and the communal eating of falafal, while leaving me in no doubt about Britain's part in the present crisis. A few days later I learned that 2 November was called 'Balfour Day' and an annual strike used to be called as a reminder of the British Government's decision in 1917 to permit Jews to create a national home in Palestine. The strike was called off when Arafat officially accepted the existence of the State of Israel 8 years ago.

When I asked Ziad why refugees, who comprised a large proportion of the Palestinian population, did not form a separate constituency and press their case on Arafat, he took me a short distance through the camp to a street almost wholly occupied by one extended family (perhaps 30 nuclear families). They were originally labourers on the land of a sheikh. They would presumably jump at the opportunity to get compensation of some hundreds of dollars per head for giving up their refugee status. On the other hand, camp dwellers like the falafal shop-owner, whose identity and hopes were still tied to the ownership of land in Israel, would settle for nothing less than Return. Huge differences like this divide Balata camp; there does not appear to be a typical refugee situation. Also, as was mentioned in a discussion in the dentists' surgery later that evening, Jordan and other countries that are hosts to the refugees would probably try to exact a price for maintaining camps inside their borders. So, maybe only a small proportion of the money would find its way into refugees' pockets.

Ziad and his friends support middle-of-the-road Fatah. They have complete trust in Arafat's leadership and feel that Hamas will enter the elections only in order to scuttle the peace process. Ziad pointed across the street to a man who owns a small tile-making business. He was once an ardent Hamas supporter but, after a long spell in an Israeli gaol, he has returned to Balata and is standing as a Fatah candidate. However, his son supports Hamas! A number of times refugees have told me in a tone of exasperation that, in the words of one Balata interviewee, 'We were the wood of the fire of revolution yet we live in such a bad condition. We were not fighting for bread or food – we had those under the Occupation – we were fighting for independence and freedom.'

The lack of employment was a major concern for Ziad: the factions are very conscious of the precarious position of many families and they try to help their supporters. He showed me a few workshops along the road that passes the camp: confectionery, flour, packaging and tiles; olive oil extraction and stone crushing; and an abattoir on the other side of a field. Looking around the camp you would think house extensions and repairs provide many jobs, but the family and friends of the owner always rally round and so money does not pass hands. Ziad believes about 50% of men have paid work in 1995. [Two years later, the figure was nearer to 40% and it fell below 20% during the frequent 'closures' imposed by Israel on all towns and villages as security measures; economic life comes virtually to a halt.] For almost 30 years the main source of work has been in Israel.

Employment in Balata Camp

UNRWA (including 100 teachers,
sanitation engineers and workers in clinics)...........................200
PNA (including 250 in security;
100 in hospitals; 50 civilians) 400
NABLUS..500
SELF-EMPLOYED in Camp
(garages, workshops, taxi-drivers)...300
TEMPORARY WORK in ISRAEL ......fluctuating around 2,500

TOTAL (maximum) 3,900

These figures were collected in September 1997 but everyone agreed that they have varied little through the nineties. The total of adult men of working age is in the region of 7,000. Thus, in 'ordinary times', 55% are in work. When a 'closure' is imposed no work is available in Israel. Those in work fall to around 1,400 or 17%.

Education was another major preoccupation in Balata. Hassan explained this intensity of interest with the remark, 'We have the time. There is so little work. We sit around all the time', though I have to set against this comment the opinion often expressed to me in Nablus that the Palestinians turned to education after 1948 in the belief that the Jews won because of the high priority they gave to education. There are many bachelors of arts in the camp and some masters of arts, though most can only find work in the Authority. When I asked young men what they suffered most during the conflict with Israel I was struck by the fervour with which many said it was the interruption to their education. The young men who were ready to leave school and were eligible for university lost the most. Ziad is convinced that the Israeli authorities deliberately took him and his uncle away for questioning on the day their school graduation exams were due to begin. He was taken away again a day or so after his final school exam. He only learned the results later when his mother visited him in prison. Ziad also missed three or four months from his An Najah studies because of the gaoling he received at the time he lost his eye.

The debilitating effect of interruptions to schooling was a theme of many younger people I spoke with: Ahmad of Fari'a camp is a case in point. Continuing our round of interviews Khalil and I arrived outside his home in mid December. He greeted us warmly and a little wearily. He had a caring face and slow, considerate manner. His voice and eyes were gentle and his hands big, coarse and friendly. His eyes looked bloodshot, as if he were under stress. Dressed differently he could have been a respected worker-priest. It was 3:00 in the afternoon and he had just left his work on a building site. In the evenings he was a sports teacher in the camp's youth club. Still in his dusty clothes, he invited us into his living room. The plaster on the walls had the smell of newness. As he talked a story of financial pressure emerged. He was born in a tent provided by UNRWA, the first son of a couple from Arab Al-Sawalma village. When he was 21 the family suffered two blows. Earnings were lost when the brother next in line died and Ahmad's UNRWA allowance was brought to an end by the completion of his vocational training. Ahmad acted quickly to repair this damage: he brought his marriage forward and set up home in a separate house. Yet, this relieved his parents of his upkeep only by transferring a burden on to the newly-weds. The traditional wedding is open to the whole community and is famously expensive: £2,000 had to be borrowed. Gone are thoughts of pursuing a skilled trade or maybe a teaching career. With three young children he takes what work he can find and feels thankful he has any.

This story is not confined to men. Rashedah is the sister in law of Ibrahim, whose family I stayed with in Gaza City in January. She joined us one evening and offered to tell me about her life. Her sharp educated mind, self-reliance, realism and commitment to the welfare of her people are immediately evident. Yet again I am struck by the failure of the stereotype of the submissive Arab woman. Rashedah will grace whatever role she finds once her part-time university study is complete. I would not be surprised if she found a place in politics. She grew up in nearby Jabalia camp and moved in to Ibrahim's house when she married one of his brothers. Now 27 and a mother, she remembers vividly as a young girl listening to her father talking about life before 1948. He was born into a small Bedouin clan and was 12 in 1948. He is still saddened when he remembers 1948 and the lack of rights and opportunities since then. He told Rashedah about his home village and its extensive lands, its stream and fresh air, and the clearly delineated seasonal round of crops and animals. 'Everything there was good; then he was rich,' she says. Rashedah still wants this land back.

She twice mentioned the value of education while talking about her father. She felt that the years he spent in school helped him to take a liberal attitude towards her role in the family. As the second of 15 children she was required to act as a second mother. Her parents gave this job to her sisters when Rashedah began to negotiate her teens. When she was a child she accepted everything – the family's situation and the explanations of it – as she found them. As an adult however she is now angered by thoughts of her family's dispossession and by the lack of education of her parents and grandparents, which, she believes, made it easy for Israel to take the land away. She is keenly aware of the way poverty has restricted the aspirations of camp dwellers. Today, she says, a Jabilia family of two parents and five children needs 450 shekels a week for the necessities of life. However, many families in the camp receive only 450 shekels *a month*. Moreover, many families have 10 or more children. And the future is bleak. Her bitter-tasting sense of realism tells her that the peace process will do nothing to put matters right, but will merely offer to the people of Jabilia some small alleviation of their physical circumstances.

Official educational resources are thinly spread; private resources are almost nonexistent. One day Ziad showed me with pride a few boxes of cheap pencils and rubbers that Fatah has bought with donations from its members for the school children. More to the point, refugee education is under acute pressure. The life choices of the generation that follows Hassan, Ahmad and Rashedah will be greatly restricted unless something is done quickly. At the outset of my stay, when I was still building up background material, I arranged to meet the UNRWA education officers who administer 41 schools for refugees in the Nablus area. UNRWA's budget is badly over-stretched. The schools cater for double the number of children they were intended for by operating morning and afternoon shifts. And now austerity has hit teachers' salaries. Newly qualified UNRWA teachers (who are paid less than those in the private or state sectors) earn about 370 shekels (£82) a week before tax – twice what a Palestinian labourer can get in Israel. Dependency allowances are given in addition; nonetheless, rent for a family flat in a good area would eat up three-quarters of the pay of a teacher on the most common career grade. The *Jerusalem Times* reports the dismay of a teacher in a government school at the prospect of retiring on about 270 shekels (£60) a week, on which he has to bring up 10 children. Young people in work often look down on teachers for undertaking a long education for small reward. I've noticed a general respect for the PhD ('Il ductuur') yet the underemployment of graduates has discounted the status of the BA. The PNA has just reported that 61% of graduates from Palestinian universities are unemployed and only 1% of those employed work in their chosen field. Demand for university places remains insatiable nonetheless! Maybe, as Hassan says, there is nothing else that offers any help to youths with time on their hands.

In education, as in so many other aspects of life, the effect of the intifada is still apparent today. Opinions are divided over its effect on teacher-pupil relations. An administrator said that children whose education was disrupted by the fighting usually came from families who were already deprived: children in these families generally left school at the earliest opportunity anyway. A counsellor pointed to the way sympathetic relationships had grown between teachers and children from families in which the father or a brother was killed, injured or imprisoned. Teachers filled some kind of need in these children. Teachers offered extra periods outside school hours. These changes drew teachers into the society of their pupils. In the early days of the intifada boys looked up to teachers and, for their part, teachers strove to prevent the fighting from affecting school life. These gains have been lost in recent years. The end of fighting has taken teachers' protective role away and the impoverishment of UNRWA has made teachers' pay look unworthy of professional workers.

The morning of my next meeting with Ziad left little time for contemplative talk. It was the 22nd of November, about 6:00 in the morning. The shaking of my bed had just woken me up. The floor shuddered as if a big dumper lorry was repeatedly driving into to the ground floor, trying to knock the building down. This seemed to go on for a few minutes; I lost track of the time. I didn't know which was the safer – to leave the building or stay in the protection of the bed. When the worst of the shuddering had stopped I got up and checked out of the window. No one was about. In my tiredness and confusion I wondered if I'd imagined things. But, I later found that two books had travelled the length of a long table, a broom fell from the flat above on to my balcony and a tile on the floor was loosened. I also learned that the earthquake, six on the Richter scale, reached from Syria to Egypt. Another tremor was expected soon. Only much later did I learn that Nablus lies on the fault line of the Great Rift Valley and this area has survived five earthquakes in this century – and *then* I remembered about the earthquake that nearly destroyed Nablus 70 years ago. There was a small tremor three days later, much milder than this one.

On the way to visit Hassan, Ziad and I passed people in the Balata alleys talking about last night's tremor. Hassan greeted us with the news that, when he left his home earlier this morning, he found a man, known to be an Israeli collaborator, lying on his doorstep shot through the knees. Word quickly spread on the camp 'grapevine' that this, the work of three men, was a lesson to others. As we settled down over cups of tea to mull over the events in the cool of Hassan's living room, his aged aunt, the daughter of a sheikh, let me know in stark, dignified terms that she saw Britain as the cause of all the troubles. She admitted that the young will probably accept jobs created by the peace process, but she was certain the old would cherish their dream of Return and remember Britain. She added that, as the daughter of a sheikh, she received a British pension, though it had to come from Amman. She agreed with a smile when I said that the British were both bad and good, and we parted on good terms.

I am picking up a strong message from residents and officials that camp life has fragmented in the last few years. This coincides ironically with the end of the intifada and the onset of the peace process. Husam Khader (his real name), who heads the Committee for the Defence of Palestinian Refugee Rights from an office in Balata camp, where he also lives, summed this up for me. 'During the first two years of the intifada people were strong and sacrificed much, they were unified and strongly identified. In those days, people closed their eyes and trusted the leadership. Now, they ask, will I get something from this political decision?' Not only is there intense competition for the local work but the political factions also compete for support. Feeling they don't get the respect that they are due from townspeople adds extra salt to their wounds. As I write in December 1999 there are reports that Arafat has just ordered 2,000 policemen to surround Balata. This show of strength was meant to force some camp leaders to give themselves up, surrender their weapons and accept the writ of the Authority. The confrontation began when members of a Balata family fought with a man related to an influential Nablus clan. The camp dwellers threatened to use the guns hidden in the camp in retribution, in an example of the continuing town-camp rivalry. Referring to the refugees and the national leadership, a Balata leader is quoted as saying, 'Fighters trigger the revolution, brave men lead it and the cowards reap its fruits.'[1] Yet some cultural values retain great tenacity. In the damp and mud of an alley in Askar Camp in Nablus a small number of passing strangers stopped and repaired the fault in Mahmoud's stricken car one evening. We had been visiting one of his friends. Mahmoud delighted in pointing out this example of comradeship to me. For him, I think, it is a distinguishing feature of camp life to set against the many aspects of decay.

Not surprisingly, attitudes to the Oslo Peace Process are changing fast. Long delays in its implementation and the economic collapse that has accompanied it have soured people's views. People are comparing the misery of life now with the pain of the exodus in the months that followed the 1967 War. And, for refugees who were at the forefront of the fighting in the intifada and took much of the punishment, the traumatic developments of the last decade have bred deep disillusion and caution. Their resettlement or compensation will be at the centre of what the Oslo Agreements

---

(1) *The Jerusalem Report*, 20 December 1999, pp 34-35.

call 'final-status' negotiations with Israel. Yet, the intifada started with a flush of national pride and communal sharing and ended in factional recriminations; the Oslo Peace Process, greeted with joy by many, has produced only pseudo-independence on a fraction of the land held in 1967, high unemployment, and a government associated with corruption and a considerable record of human rights abuses against its own people. Many younger men now see the intifada as a failure; some regret the time they took from school or college. One man now in the security service told me he accepted responsibility for this – no word against Israel here – he has moved on. Jewish attitudes towards education have become a totem to many Palestinians, promising personal fulfilment and national salvation. An awareness of the previous generation's lack of schooling makes the interruptions experienced by people now in their 20s and 30s particularly galling. Many personal re-appraisals have taken place against a background of the failing peace process, which was itself perhaps the chief fruit of the intifada. Few older refugees I spoke with will settle for less than return to the villages in present-day Israel where they grew up; more of the young people will settle for a return to the pre-1967 situation. But they are tired and angry. I listened to a moving expression of this on my next visit.

The Camp's lights have just failed twice but we continue talking by candlelight. There is a dispute with the Israeli Electricity Company over payments. Hassan is to become a policeman based in Nablus. He has a gentle face and manner but a band of steel runs through his thinking. His English seems to have regressed since we first met. Ziad and his uncle are students; neither has married. Ziad's mother jokes about this but I think she is more concerned than the tone of her voice suggests. How many other men have delayed their marriages and changed their life expectations? In the weak light I asked both men about their feelings for the past. Hassan replied, 'The old men tell us every day about life in the villages before 1948. We have many stories from then. My family has a certificate of ownership of our land.' Ziad echoed these sentiments: 'My grandfather speaks of this every day.' Hassan took up the issue of Return, re-iterating its centrality in Palestinian thinking. It would be difficult to implement but, he adds, 'living here is difficult too.' No one knows what will happen when the Balata lease runs out soon. Things are getting worse. 'People were united during the intifada, not like now. A problem was a problem for all, not separately for Fatah or Hamas. The Israeli soldiers were against all of us, not one or some. We gave everything – blood, food for a neighbour. It is difficult now. Everyone wants work. We want peace. We don't like fighting. But we have a feeling the Israelis don't really want peace. We want to talk, but every day an Israeli settlement is expanded, someone is killed. Why does Hamas make explosions every day? Do they *like* to kill?'

Ziad took up the thread: 'We respected Peres and Rabin, and fear Netanyahu. Every day is bad now, there are no good periods. Every time I travel to Ramallah I am questioned by Israeli soldiers with lists of wanted men.' Hassan was pragmatic. 'We do not want the land occupied in 1948. To resolve the problem here Netanyahu must give us back the land taken after the 1967 war. But every day sees settlements expanding on it.' I sought clarification – they, the younger generation, might be happy with land held before the 1967 War, but what about their fathers? Without thinking, Hassan replied, 'Believe me, he cries.' Ziad quickly expanded on this point, 'You know that Germany gives Israel money every year. I want to go to my land of 1948 and I want to receive money for 50 years living in tents and in the camp.' Then he seemed to drift away. 'You know, the life of the camps –the streets, the housing, the medicine and the schools – is very, very difficult. I am 28 years old; seven years I lost because of Israeli soldiers. The soldier shot me in the eye and leg. This is a very, very big problem for me. I remember every day, every day, when I look in the mirror. The Israelis get money from Germany. When the Israeli soldier shot me in the eye he must pay for it.' Hassan was thinking along the same lines. 'The soldiers came in the middle of the night in the prison and punished me. We do not ask for a good life, only a simple one.' Seeking for some light in the dark, I asked, 'Do you feel freer now the Israelis have left Nablus?' Hassan replied wearily, as if talking to a novice, 'Freedom, no. In the camp, yes, but I walk with you just five minutes and we will see a soldier. And there is a line and beyond that he can do anything, he punishes and...What peace? That's peace? Not peace.'

This strikes a cord. I stop writing and look around for a recent edition of *The Return Review*. It reports that Fari'a spring is under threat – and with it the camp's water supply. The culprit is not an Israeli but a newly-rich refugee. Plans to develop the area threaten the villagers' use of the spring and some adjacent land. The *Review* went on: 'With feelings evidently running high, Fari'a camp residents are asking whether this is the reward for their resistance and long struggle against foreign occupation.' While they wait in trepidation to find how the final-status negotiations will affect them, the refugee community is suffering internal blows as some of its members try to climb on the shoulders of others. The clan system (and its modifications in the camp) stands in opposition to such extreme individualism. The clans and the camp are geared to the exigencies of another world. Ironically their philosophy has more in common with that of a kibbutz than with capitalism. Will the Authority intercede? It's very unlikely. They want enterprise to succeed. Presumably they hope the whole refugee issue will be resolved in the revived peace process. And they have to juggle many balls, two of which are the traditional and modernising elements in Palestinian society.

I remember being puzzled quite early on by the frequent use of the word 'poverty'. People mention it all the time in the camps. Yet, an old man who was classified as an UNRWA 'special case' because he had no resources, also reminded me of the bad times before the Uprooting of 1948. Today, discontent often focuses on economic deprivation. Well-being is measured against the condition of neighbouring groups; for rural Fari'a camp this means farmers in the nearby village. It invariably seems to be the known and measurable; comparisons with Israel or the West are rare. Poverty, by any standard, is widespread. But other issues at stake include expulsion, degradation and lack of sovereignty. Poverty seems to act as a kind of shorthand for these complex feelings.

I've got used to falling into conversation with men in the street; social and religious conventions make this difficult with women. Men want to talk about my response to Palestinian travails or about the world situation (and probably, to practise their English). I met one young man yesterday and we chatted for some while as we crossed the town. We met again today by chance as we walked in a large crowd of men to a celebration of the independence of Nablus from Israeli troops, which Arafat is addressing. He is to hold the weekly cabinet meeting here after this event. We gathered in a large square on the edge of town. A gaol for political prisoners, only just abandoned by Israeli soldiers, took up one side of the square. After nearly an hour two helicopters circled and descended into the grounds of the gaol, while another of a different design continued hovering high above. 'These are Arafat's helicopters, they are lent by Egypt for ceremonial occasions,' my friend said. 'The other is Israeli. They never let him out of their sight.' Soon Arafat's voice echoed through the public address system, 'there he is,' said someone, pointing to the roof of the gaol, 'that is his hand.' Everyone round me stared into the glare of the sun that came directly from above the gaol. We had waited an hour for this moment. Yet, high above us, surrounded by his soldiers and in front of many thousands of his own people, Arafat hid behind his lieutenants, revealing only a waving hand to the crowd. As the crowd dispersed in twos and threes there was a noticeable absence of anything suggesting a feeling of celebration. A few days later, a teacher in Fari'a camp told me that virtually all the 40,000 people who turned out to hear Arafat today were refugees. Yet Arafat's speech didn't once mention them or their efforts during the intifada, though he fulsomely praised the fortitude of the townsfolk.

CHAPTER 7

Walid

English friends wanted to give me a treat and took me to a remote spot in the Pennines. They pointed out with pride that we had left the city crowds behind, 'Look, there is not a person in sight!' In astonishment I replied, 'I appreciate your kindness, but there is nothing for me here. As an Arab I like to be among people, the more crowded and noisy the better!'

Walid

IN MID NOVEMBER Walid, a fellow student of Ziad's, invited me to stay with his family. Walid is a dashing and debonair man of about 28. He has the sort of demeanour that in my ignorance I might expect of a Bedouin, though he is in fact from old West Bank farming stock. Outgoing and alert, he carries a natural authority in the circles where we meet. The fact that he is a devout Muslim does not stop him cutting a dash. We spent yesterday in Nablus and in and around his village. As we made our way to the taxi to take us over Mt Ebal, we noticed that older schoolchildren were moving towards the Israeli police and army station on the main street. There, youths were throwing stones at the building and at some soldiers. The soldiers retaliated by firing tear gas and chasing the young men down the nearby Street of Goldsmiths into the market area. It is only two days until the Israeli troops are due to leave Nablus. Later, in Walid's village, we learned that 40 youths were injured and one killed by Israeli troops in Nablus and two nearby villages. The prevailing view was that the agitation occurred because Israel delayed the release of political prisoners.

Walid lives in a beautiful old stone house, sparsely furnished in the Arab style, near the mosque and the centre of this hill village, which seemed to be sleeping in the stark midday sunlight when I arrived. From about 6:00 in the evening, after the main meal of the day was finished, I 'promenaded' with Walid and his friends and neighbours along the main streets of the village. To and fro and then back again and the wave-like movement of the people around me created a feeling I'd rarely experienced before, of being part of a great communal event carrying me along benevolently in its breast. In twos and threes the (usually) younger men conversed as the sun set, and I watched my footsteps on the uneven ground by light from the doorways of open shops. Then, back for tea and cakes with the family, some television and bed.

Walid has many brothers, one of whom works for the PLO. He hopes to follow in his brother's footsteps. However widely the family disperses everyone returns to the family home for a few months once in a while. Like Ziad, Walid wanted me to look through his family photographs with a close friend. The family story might be exceptional because of its career successes, but it is nonetheless typically clouded by conflict with occupiers, British and Israeli. Walid's grandfather died at the hands of the British, I didn't enquire why. The family owns the house next door, which lies in ruins, demolished by Israelis troops because of the family's involvement in the resistance. At least two brothers have spent time in Israeli gaols, one for about six years. Is there a family not affected like this?

The West Bank has a grip on the imagination of everyone I get close to. The remarks of Khalil, Mahmoud and Ziad are punctuated with loving references to their land, as are Walid's now, even though he would like to work abroad. It amounts to more than possession of the land or of some sort of nationalism. I hear it as an expression of yearning to be connected to something eternal and loving. It is conveyed in the word *baladi* (my land). Khalil made this point strongly when he spoke emotionally of *Bilad as Shaam*, the land of the people of old Greater Syria, and of his attachment to his own town. Land is expensive in the village, Walid said, because people in Nablus want to move to this beautiful, timeless spot on the edge of the mountain. Attachment to village land is ingrained in the hearts of families here. Jewish attempts to move into the village have always been repulsed. In the patriotic and strained atmosphere of the intifada, anyone found to have sold land to Jews, whatever their need for money, was shot, a fate similar to that handed out to collaborators in the camps.

Walking with Walid through olive groves above the village I saw Fari'a camp in the far distance. The narrow valley it occupies is a speck of green in the wide landscape of fawn rocks and white, stony ground that stretches to the mountains of Jordan on the horizon. How different from the constricted and congested views of the camps near Nablus! We stopped to chat with two local farmers who gave me a glimpse into the nature of a rural economy subject to tight Israeli controls. They wanted to show me that some farmers are self-sufficient in foodstuffs and can withstand a closure. They pointed to their stocks of produce as proof. I think a lot of patriotic pride is at work here yet I realised that there is a limit, although a very harsh one, to the harm a closure can do to the rural economy of the West Bank. A large proportion of West Bankers still live on the land – this is a third world economy – and stockpiling might be easy to do from one season to the next, when the rainfall holds up. Farmers who export their produce can suffer badly – a particular problem for the orange and flower growers of Gaza – but it is the urban sector that suffers most. The cost of living immediately goes up and they become even more dependent than before on Israeli processed food. The Palestinian National Authority is powerless to help.

We visited the house of an aunt and found her talking with two friends in a garden of orange and almond trees. She has just returned from the Pilgrimage to Mecca (hajj*)* and has put some dyestuff on her hands in recognition. I asked a young Orthodox female relative if I might take her picture but she refused. In some embarrassment I instead photographed a donkey standing inside the garden wall, and only then plucked up courage to ask Walid if his aunt and her friends would object to me taking them. They said that they had been waiting to be asked and thought I had given priority to the donkey. On Fridays Walid's father usually walks over his fields for the sheer joy he gets looking at the land. As today is the Holy Day he will not work, instead, Walid says with a smile, 'he will probably talk to his donkeys.'

Walking together across the city centre one day he mentioned how much cleaner it was since Arafat installed a new mayor. Many people initially saw the mayor as a crony of Arafat, yet he has proved, admittedly in a high-handed way, that he wants to put a new face on the city. In the past, perpetual squabbles incapacitated the baladiyya (council). As we waited for a taxi to take Walid home, I realise it was on this spot only three days ago that we noticed that a stone-throwing incident was brewing. I also remember how strange it felt to see everyone except the youths and soldiers carrying on with their ordinary business. I doubt my memory for a moment – the square seems so innocent of that incident now.

Walid is pessimistic about the future. He quoted the Koran to the effect that everyone should love and worship freely and in harmony. Yet, at the Day of Judgement, after the Jews have gained power, abused it and sunk, like any great empire, Islam would rise again. Muslims should be watchful, for the stones will speak of a Jew hiding and ready to kill a Muslim and, when his life is threatened, a Muslim has the right to kill a Jew. Walid said he didn't think Muslims and Jews would ever be able to live together. He agreed when I suggested that reconciliation work like that carried out at Beit Sahour could be valuable. But he felt it would offer more hope if it was organised by neutral or Christian bodies and if ordinary people took a bigger part.

Later, in the student refectory, Walid again reminded me of the urgent need for a return to Islamic teachings and values. I find it very difficult to reconcile Walid's love of smart clothes and dashing manner with his strong religious beliefs. He admitted that many young people are rejecting Islam because they believe it is holding up the modernisation of the country. They want the material benefits and personal freedom that western styles of living seem to offer. Walid felt this attitude would lead to spiritual and social perdition. The Koran offers all the advice needed to lead a mature and fulfilling life.

A day or two later Walid gave me some worrying news. Someone in Hamas who was involved in a bus attack in Israel was killed in Gaza yesterday. Hamas and Fatah immediately called for a strike. Walid was depressed because today's empty streets took him right back to the days of the intifada. He said the killing raises some awkward questions. Apparently, an explosive device was planted in the man's mobile phone, which virtually never left his hands. This points to someone very close to him. Also, for the Israeli secret agents to get so near to him, in Gaza of all places, in the compact communities where Hamas has such a strong appeal, suggests the connivance of the Palestinian National Authority. Alternatively, the Palestinian security service is badly out of touch with events. Either way people are worried and want an explanation. Did the Israeli security service not see this could turn people against the peace process? Or did they argue that the Palestinians have no other course to follow and would have to stomach the death of one of their heroes? The record of the Israeli security service suggests they could have planned for the emergence of anti-PNA feelings. This may weaken the Palestinian position in the negotiations. Popular doubts about Arafat and the PNA in this affair could diminish the Authority's standing and strengthen a not uncommon belief that Arafat is acting like an Israeli stooge. So, Arafat's record on human and civil rights is under the spotlight once again. Walid also feared that, once the strike ends, the effect of this Israeli action would be to deepen the political estrangement of Fatah and Hamas. National energies would be wasted on internal feuds. Israel and the militant Islamists might sanction armed attacks on each other again.

I'm left wondering about the decisions made inside the Israeli security services that led to this killing. Closing down one source of the bombs in an area under Palestinian control where militant Islam is strong was given priority over the promise of long-term peace that might flow from the Oslo process. Do they believe in Oslo? I am beginning to get some sense of the depth of pain in Israel. This death removes a major Israeli target, yet we have just reached the most delicate point in the peace process in the sobering aftermath of Rabin's assassination. Some Palestinians who retain their trust in Arafat (despite the disquieting evidence of doubtful judgements and anti-libertarian tendencies) can admit in an aside that the naked weakness of their representatives is a sobering portent for the future.

CHAPTER 8

Ruth and Afif

I am meeting people who are dissatisfied with old political dogmas. More often than not, they locate the real problems as much in the rigid, old ways of thinking on their own side as in the slogans and behaviour of the opposing camp.

FOR THE MOMENT the atmosphere seems to be freeing up as the joint Israeli-Palestinian patrols get underway near Nablus: checks at the roadblocks seem peremptory. I spent the morning photographing the dignified Ottoman houses in Jerusalem's Jaffa Road area. People looked relaxed there too.

RUTH

I talked with Ruth over lunch in a Jerusalem café. She and her husband came to Israel many years ago to express their sympathy with fellow Jews. She supports Peace Now, an Israeli group formed in 1978 to oppose the Israeli attack on Lebanon. Peace Now favours giving independence and land to the Palestinians. Ruth also supports Meretz, a left-wing party forced to stay on the sidelines because the establishment Labour Party is in thrall to the religious Right, whose support it needs to sustain its appeal across the political spectrum. As a result, she says, Labour is little different from Likud. Meretz is a lone voice recognising the Palestinian case, so the peace process inches forward hesitantly. She took up reconciliation work during the early days of the intifada.

Ruth is a quietly attractive and contained woman who, despite her active peace work, seems a reticent person. Perhaps I am unfair to her. I have this very morning travelled the short distance from a totally different world to this one in Israel. I have come with the intention of facing her with my strong criticisms of Israel's record and see her in some way as a representative of the Israeli stance. It is difficult to get angry with this quietly spoken, concerned woman. She was guarded at first, not smiling unaffectedly for some time. I warned her of my critical attitude. She seemed to accept this, but she veered away from some questions. One concerned the unequal number of people killed and injured on the two sides. When I said this was appalling she was clearly stung and asked about Israelis killed by Hizbulla in northern Israel and Lebanon.

She generally took a philosophical, even deterministic view of the conflict when I asked her if she can see a way through: 'This is a generation that has lost out, some are born to lose. It is the poor who suffer in both countries.' She is angry with the PLO: 'There is a lot of money in the PLO. Why does it go on such a large army? We must make sure the Palestinian refugees get some of the money going into Palestine.' A socialist concern for the disadvantaged on both sides ran through her comments; she saw many problems as common to the two peoples. 'The people who are suffering most in Israel – similar in some ways to the refugees in Palestine – are in the development towns of the Negev.' She thought the intifada was a watershed in relations: 'There was a lot of intermingling before the intifada, at least for workers and servants...Our peace group was formed when the barriers began to rise between the two peoples during the intifada.'

She was hopeful of the outcome of the forthcoming Israeli election. 'Peres and Labour will sweep the board...and will push the Peace Process...Even now people on both sides in the peace group are explaining their internal issues rather than getting worked up about the actions of the other side... The extreme Zionists are a small proportion of the population...the settlement movement will lose its momentum and joint Israeli-Palestinian enterprises will become possible in time...the settlements will stay in their present form only if the PLO abdicates its power.'

When I arrived back in the flat John said the election process was working well; only one or two cases of corruption have emerged. It is clear, however, that the short run-up to the election has created problems. Broadcasting times for candidates and parties have not been distributed fairly and media treatment massively favours Fatah. Groups like refugees and women are badly under-represented whereas Christians and Samaritans have their own seats protected by a quota system. On Arafat's orders the Samaritans were allotted a seat for their 400 or so members; four candidates are contesting it.

AFIF

One evening I invited Walid and his friends Afif and Mousa to the flat. Walid offered to cook a meal with his own supplies of herbs and spices and fresh salad. This was the entrée to another evening of intense political and social debate.

Afif told me of his frustration with the speed of social change. He complained of the power that parents possess. Boys and girls may not touch and sometimes dare not speak together before marriage. He realised nonetheless, that young men were selective in their irritation with old customs. On the one hand, they want some of the freedoms associated with the West, like going out with girls and being more independent of their parents. On the other, they want to hold on to the tradition of taking their new brides back to live with them in their village of origin. At the same time, Afif pointed out, women may seem independent in the precincts and courtyards of the university (where they are about half the student population) or in city streets, but they immediately become deferential to parents or husband once inside home. Only the rich, he contended, who give a nod to Islam and yet drink and are free with marriage vows and sexual mores, have really broken with tradition.

Afif and Walid agreed that Israel is no longer the main enemy. They believe the biggest problem is now the gap between the leading families and the rest of society. The middle classes tend to follow rather than direct the political current. The masses do not know what they want of politics – long hours of work or boredom resulting from unemployment and little education make them seek comfort. Politicians offer grandiose dreams in a world of infinitely tiny possibilities. This conversation gave me pause for thought, for it was the first time I'd heard class singled out as one of the chief causes of Palestinian troubles. Thus far I'd identified it only in the guise of resentment against the wealth and power of the new elite of returnees from Tunis.

CHAPTER 9

Ibrahim and Mona

We are all refugees in Gaza. *Ibrahim*

THE SNOW THAT covered Jerusalem gives way to rain and then to tepid warmth as the taxi nears the border with Gaza at Erez. It is mid January now and as cold as it is going to be. I wait with a small crowd of Palestinian workers in rough clothes, some Arabs and others in well-cut clothes and one or two back-packers at the Israeli post, until they call us through. I walk a little way along a flimsy boarded alleyway past three very young soldiers who were totally involved in a piece of horse-play, finding it difficult to hide my distaste with their behaviour. One of them, a boy of no more than 18, turns and shouts something to me in what I presume is Hebrew. I realise from his gestures he wants me to walk back to him. I resent acting at his beck and call in this undignified way. I said, 'I've walked past you once.' He doesn't respond, takes a cursory look in my bag without emptying it and says something with a dismissive tone. I walked away wondering how I could possibly stand this or something worse every day. I am protected by my passport. How might a Palestinian labourer fare though, who was dependent on his daily work in Israel?

Having crossed the bleak, open wasteland that separates the two checkpoints I was approached by a Palestinian police officer who offered me his hand and enquired, 'Dr Roy?' Before I had time to make sense of what was happening he took me to where Mona, my hostess, was waiting in her car. She had asked him to look out for me. She is small and bustlingly energetic and smiles a lot. In the car, greetings completed, she drove into Gaza City, weaving effortlessly between oncoming traffic and pedestrians. We narrowly avoided a pedestrian and a cyclist when the car mounted the road verge. I assumed this was a pedestrian walkway in normal times; now it is invisible beneath a foot or more of water. The wide main road is an impossible river of deep, fast moving floodwater whose flow is impeded only by small, sharp-sided islands of sand. I later learned that the rainwater has mixed with the overflow from the sewage system to create this incongruous and noxious seascape.

Mona's husband Ibrahim commands attention – he is stocky and bearded and formally dressed, his eyes fix me with a strong gaze as he speaks. Although always an extremely caring and occasionally light-hearted host, he almost always spoke from a deep well of experience and learning regarding the fate of his people. But his first words were about my recent journey as he explained that the poor physical infrastructure, illustrated by the condition of the roads, raises the expense of owning a car. Car suspensions collapse quickly on these pitted sand and mud 'roads'. Yet, the *capital* cost of a car is low. Mona obtained her car cheaply because it was originally stolen in Israel. This widespread practice makes it easier to acquire a modern car. The disposal in Gaza of cars stolen by Israeli thieves was a large, well-established trade till the Israel authorities stepped in recently. Most of the cars privately owned by members of the Palestinian security service are Israeli 'imports'.

Over the next few days our conversation kept returning to political issues. Ibrahim spoke of Arafat's ways of dealing with rivals. The first entailed turning challengers into 'consultants'. He makes an issue of asking for advice, listens to it and then ignores it. The second device is called 'broken eyes'. [When someone wants to say he has vanquished someone else in this part of the Arab world, he says, 'I broke his eyes.'] If Arafat catches someone with his hand in the till or working against him he tells the man off and then says, 'We all make mistakes, it's OK, go back to your job.' But the man knows now that he will never be able to blow the whistle or criticise Arafat. Ibrahim believes there is much corruption in the Authority. All the PLO fighters have come back from Tunis and gone straight into good jobs in the police or administration. It is not clear how the Authority's money is spent. It has as much money as Israel. Yet there is no infrastructure. 'We need time as much as

Gaza city. Street scene after January rain.

Rooftops in Gaza city.

money.' Ibrahim prefers improvement to be slow because it then tends to be real and allows time for changes to be assimilated. He is concerned that people do not know their rights or the usual channels through which to complain and are unsure how to assert themselves. Social expectations are low. He explains this by reference to the centuries that Palestinians have been occupied by other nations. The lack of forward drive is linked to a lack of open-ended, critical thinking in education. Moreover, leaders do not expect to suffer criticism or competition. Rivals are seen as enemies who must be removed instead of as putative leaders whose striving for power will keep the present leaders on their toes.

It is Friday and Ibrahim is praying. I am in a lively family environment. It is difficult to realise I go home soon. Gaza City is outside but my only connections with it are the sounds of the muessin and of the persistent patter of rain. I was invited by little Hanan to see the sheep being kept downstairs next to the front-door porch. It will be sacrificed in a day or so to welcome a new baby into the extended family and celebrate the return of two family friends (arrested in this house) who have been released by Israel (as part of the peace process) after two or three years of their 10 year sentences. I said I couldn't bear to witness the sheep being killed and the family accepted this. My first impression of Gaza City yesterday was of a ramshackle main street flowing in places with a foot or more of water traversed by cars and donkey-drawn carts and (the side-roads) by occasional Heath-Robinson, wooden footbridges. Today I see that the side roads are sandy undulations as well. Looking across the City skyline from the top of Ibrahim's three-storey house I can see activity on many other rooftops. It is strangely intimate, a speaking voice distance away – washing hanging and people standing or working. Buildings stretch to the horizon, one roof space linking with the next, like many rooms in one limitless house. From the roof of Ibrahim's house his brother is shouting – he wants me to see the chickens, pigeons and rabbits he keeps up there for food.

A majority of the people of Gaza are refugees. This thought made me ask Ibrahim if the refugees have a political voice here. He replied that 'everyone speaks for refugees and we don't like to talk about them as if they are set apart from the rest. We share the same situation.' I had wanted a response to my belief that the refugees would benefit from representation as a constituency (which I raised with Ziad and Hassan in Balata). But, having just left the West Bank where the refugees are a minority, albeit a large one, of the population, I had forgotten the dominance of the refugee voice here in Gaza. Moreover the typical refugee on the West Bank dwells in a town where a degree of assimilation has occurred, and town refugees outnumber camp refugees. The latter are only one voice in West Bank society. In this sense Mahmoud's father who left a camp to settle in Nablus is more typical of West Bank refugees than Ziad's father who remains in Balata camp. In Gaza the reverse is true. A majority of Gazan refugees live in camps where they constitute a strong voice in the society of the Strip. This disposition affects all other Gazans. As Ibrahim said, even the relatively few Gazans who live urban professional lives and can speak the political language of the West gain infinitely greater political meaning in their lives from the cataclysmic events of 1948 and 1967. Clearly, all kinds of social and personal factors determine whether a refugee lives in a town or a camp, not only the possession of business acumen and other personality traits but, for example, whether the refugee owned land before 1948. In the latter case he is more likely to want to hold on to his UNRWA card in the hope of returning to his previous life. To become established in his town of adoption would seem like rejecting his birthright. On top of all these personal imponderables is the massive economic barrier that militates against personal advancement anyway, especially in poverty-stricken Gaza. In this sense, well-established burghers, like Mahmoud's father, back in Nablus, are very untypical of the struggling refugee community at large, whether in camps or towns. And, a Gazan professional worker like Ibrahim, who lives outside the camps, sees himself as much an integral part of refugee society as does a West Bank dentist like Zakkaria who chooses to stay in Balata camp. This may say something about the significantly different attitudes in Gaza and the West Bank as well as the personal circumstances of these men.

Ibrahim talked of the resistance to the Occupation. The two brothers released from prison had killed maybe 20 collaborators between them. There were many collaborators because conditions were so bad. 'We have many needs: money, permission to build a house, a woman. A man would kill a collaborator and the courts would give him 20 years on top of his present 50 years term, or 50 on top of 100. So what is another 50 years? Inside prison we controlled our own lives. We were put into sections, say 20 men, and no one dare enter or we'd have killed them. We had an hour or two of exercise, talking, and then the section time'.

This is the day we have been waiting for – Saturday 20th January (yoom al-intikhab), the first General Election in Palestinian history. After a shopping visit to a street market in the city centre I went with all the family to visit Beach Camp. Ibrahim wanted me to see a local camp and, though tired by my interviews, I did not want to disappoint him. Although it seems small, Beach Camp has the same regular lines, narrow alleys, bare houses and overcrowding I'm familiar with in camps in and around Nablus. We visited a kind of high-class beachcomber who sells coins and other metal and stone artefacts from a variety of periods. Despite the high prices at which he starts the haggling over these mementoes, this man lives in a house indistinguishable from his neighbours. Afterwards we walked out of the seaward side of the camp on to a beach that would be the envy of tourist boards in seaside resorts of Europe. It is empty but for a few children who have wandered from the camp. Egypt is just a few miles to the south.

I've just realised that I now feel less sad when meeting families of poor refugees. Maybe I'm getting used to the fact of the camps. I also feel a deadening mental pressure after talking to many people who suffer an acute lack of opportunity to express themselves. It is difficult to distinguish gradations of poverty by sight alone. Beach Camp raised in me the same feelings that I get in Balata – a deepening incomprehension the longer I stay there. But at least I know some people in Balata and can in however small a degree relate the exterior of their lives to their hopes, their moods and humour.

There are big differences in the cost and quality of housing within Gaza City. Near the sea and only a little way south of where we are standing outside Beach Camp, I can see an area of large houses which Ibrahim estimates cost £660,000 each. He says they are mostly occupied by leading members of the PLO who have recently returned from exile in Tunis. *The Jerusalem Times* reckons a high-rise flat costs £33,000-£40,000 to buy in some areas, £67,000 in others, mostly because land can cost up to £1m a dunum (a dunum equals a quarter of an acre). And this is in a town where the average income is £100-£200 a month! By contrast, it is possible to rent a city-centre flat of four bedrooms for only £130-£170 a month, much below what you are asked in Nablus. I wonder if the lack of middle grade jobs and the riches of the top PLO people in Gaza account for this unusually wide gap between the top and middle of the housing market.

Cynicism surrounds the contest for the Presidency between Sameeha Khalil, a 70 years old grandmother and social activist, and Arafat. According to Ibrahim she is happy to have created a contest (or the show of one) for the Presidency. Because of her age she doesn't fear recriminations for challenging Arafat. Mona admitted to being very excited, no – disturbed, by tomorrow's election. She may not sleep – it is as bad as sitting an exam. There will be dancing in the streets. She is considering visiting relatives and friends after the results are known. She expects the election to cause trouble between some individuals, but it seems very peaceful so far.

In the evening I went with adults from the extended family to two polling booths. There was a quiet atmosphere as if people wanted to savour the meaning of what they were experiencing. Much talking, though subdued. A few people took me for a European Election Observer but only wanted to chat, except for one agitated man who wanted me to explain the complexities of the voting list. As the conversation progressed later in the evening Mona told me that it is considered bad in Gaza for a woman to perform in films or to dance in public. If a girl were discovered dancing, she would be punished by her brothers. If she appeared in a film, she would be spurned rather than punished. Before we went to bed Ibrahim asked me if I'd like to wake before 3:30 in the morning and take a last meal before Ramadan. Faced with a tiring journey in the morning I declined although, wanting to honour in some way the spirit of the family's commitment, I will fast till I get to Jerusalem.

The next day I was back in my flat by late afternoon. Thunderous sounds of rifle fire and drumbeats rose from the dark streets below as evening drew on. Maybe the election results are out for the Council, or more prisoners have been released. The result of the Presidential election was announced earlier. Arafat got in, of course, with 88% of the vote. It seems likely that Fatah will take over 80% of the Council seats.

I pondered the political situation, which is now in frustrating limbo. The second stage of Oslo is successfully implemented: most of Gaza and patches of the West Bank are under Palestinian civil authority. The election was an undoubted success. The President of the executive branch and the Legislative Council have been chosen in open elections and a constitution is in the offing. Fatah swept the board but this almost certainly reflects the wishes of the people. Arafat's dictatorial tendencies auger badly but he is father of the people in most people's eyes. Unemployment has leapt up however and would be catastrophic if it were not for the employment-creating capacity of the large police force and civil administration. But where do we go from here? Until the Israeli voters chose between Peres and Netanyahu there is stasis. Cynicism is rife in the circles in which I move. Everyone knows the pace of settlement building was maintained or even increased under Rabin, even though peace was the byword. Now there is the prospect of a man coming to power whose main plank in the coming Israeli election is to throw Oslo out. Yet, there is distrust of Peres too: I've heard him described as devious – the onslaught on Lebanon he authorised is in recent memory – and I heard a preference for Netanyahu expressed because 'you know where you are with him'!

Soon I am back in Jerusalem again, for one last visit. It is a time for saying farewells. I am tying things up now and realise I have only a slight sense of the Israeli predicament. It is early afternoon and I am waiting to meet Ruth again in a café in the German Colony. Earlier I walked along a newly constructed 'Promenade' above the Kidron Valley. The gardens are imaginatively designed and maintained; the expense must be immense. To the south of the Old City a pink radiance touched everything and the buildings are the colour of sand. Sitting here in this attractive example of Israeli café society at this very moment I feel at one with life. If this café were the peace process I would be truly encouraged – small and intimate, a little dingy around the edges, prices within the reach of most people and the clientele looking contemplative and urbane.

After an hour it is clear we have muddled the times or something has happened and Ruth is not coming. I'm disappointed, but I like it at this spot in this moment. The scale of the aches, hopes, pain and magnificence of the world I inhabit here expands the meaning of everything and adds a slew of poignancy to it. I'll order another coffee and people-watch a little longer.

The next day I flew back to the UK.

CHAPTER 10

Newcastle

LIFE IN THE UK *feels flat. Whatever ingredient I found among the Palestinians that in Nadine Gordimer's words, 'released me and made me more myself' has vanished since my return. Everything here is settled, taking in only an Anglo-Saxon perspective. Large headlines shout about what strike me as the most banal of matters. Why does no one appreciate the great moral and human issues that have so recently reverberated through my daily life? It's only an air flight away. If I expostulate, people back away. The universal issues that feature in the daily lives of Israelis and Palestinians are perceived here only in terms of a local, incomprehensible conflict, given only a limited amount of the residual attention left after the day's work or watching the TV news slot.*

There, things are going from bad to worse. Eight months after my departure I read with horror of gun battles erupting across the West Bank and Gaza. Palestinians were inflamed by Netanyahu's decision to open a tunnel under the Al-Aqsa mosque in Jerusalem. About 40 Israeli soldiers and settlers were besieged at Joseph's Tomb near Balata camp and six Israeli soldiers were killed there in a day's fighting. The Palestinian authorities imposed a curfew so the Israelis could withdraw. On the phone Khalil is always his usual cheery self for the first few minutes, but gloom and cynicism creep in if we talk for long.

My stay has put me in touch with something I want. Yet it looks as if it can be acquired only by having the double advantage of being an expert and an outsider. If so, these are dubious advantages. There is always a danger of romanticising my place there – some kind of western technocratic benefactor. There must be something better, a different reality. What is it in the here-and-now that is so difficult to accept? Maybe something to do with the quality of attention to daily living, with staying in each minute, feeling every feeling, doing things only when necessary, enjoying life unravelling at its own pace, unprovoked by extravagant expectations?

Nonetheless I feel a growing desire to return to the West Bank. Is this clutching at excitement, at what I know thrills me? The pull of eastern culture is certainly a consideration. But the desire to complete the project is growing too – my conscience (and some guilt) and perhaps a strengthening sense of commitment are working overtime! And nothing else offers so much meaning as being present among the colourful absolutes of the Middle East. Will this awareness make a second trip different?

CHAPTER 11

Nablus, September 1997

The utter irony that I – with a passport, money in the bank, a vote in a democracy and some freedom to air my views, all the things Palestinians desire – find something I want here among the repression and poverty. It has something to do with a groundedness, an energy beyond mere endurance, enfolded by family life.

I AM SITTING IN my old chair at my old desk again! I have a powerful sense of déjà vu, or indeed a sense of never having left here. And Khalil has found me a lovely one-room flat in the grounds of a large house which fronts onto a busy residential street very near the centre of town. Sun drenches my northwest-facing windows soon after midday. To get to the flat I leave the street through a large wrought iron gate set in a stone frame, which demarcates a line of privacy even if it doesn't, thank heaven, stop street sounds (and the occasional debris) passing through. There is some kind of security system at the entrance, but it seems to be disdained by the residents of the 'big house' above and the gate usually stands ajar. Across the street, partly surrounded by a stone wall, is an old building, which I eventually learn belongs to the French Cultural Centre and which is enclosed by a tranquil garden.

I soon discovered that others' lives have moved on. Mahmoud has left the family restaurant for America where he is managing his father's interests. Ziad and his uncle have graduated and Ziad goes every day from Balata camp to an office job in the Palestinian National Authority in Ramallah. His friend Hassan is now a policeman. He has had to neglect his studies because his father's illness forced him to find work. His job involves patrolling the nearby hills, often during the cold nights, looking for armed Israeli settlers who periodically attack the outskirts of the town. For this he is paid $25 a week; there is not enough for the needs both of his family and himself. 'What can I do with this?' he asks with an empty expression.

In the 18 months I've been away, the peace process has become a grotesque misnomer. In the run-up to the Israeli elections that followed Rabin's assassination by an Israeli religious extremist in November 1995, the Prime Minister, Shimon Peres, made two decisions that still weigh heavily on the political future of the whole region. It must be presumed that he endorsed his secret service's assassination of the Hamas bomb-maker, Yahya Ayyash, and he ordered an attack on southern Lebanon where pockets of Hizbulla (Shi'ite Muslim) forces are concentrated. Israeli troops shelled a UN compound in the village of Qana (where Jesus turned water into wine) in Lebanon. Shi'ite Muslim refugees were sheltering there from the Israeli bombardment (called Grapes of Wrath), and 106 civilians, including 55 children, were killed. Arab anger and desire for vengeance spilled over. Suicide bombers struck back, taking 63 lives on the streets of Israel in under two weeks. The ferocious attack on Lebanon seems to have been authorised by Peres in an attempt to give a tough message to bombers and guerrillas and to head off Netanyahu's hard-line challenge for the premiership. The resulting Arab violence seems to have pushed enough voters over to Netanyahu to eat up Peres' hitherto comfortable lead in the polls. Immediately following his success in the summer of 1996, Netanyahu started to delay the implementation of Oslo and announced the building of new settlements and expansion of others on land confiscated from Arabs. Reports say some 10,000 acres have been appropriated in the first eight months of 1997. A new settlement is to join others surrounding Nablus.

It is my third day back and I am enjoying the conviviality of Daoud's family in his home in the wall of Nablus's Old City. After lunch our conversation is interrupted by a newsflash on the television screen – bombs have exploded maybe half an hour ago in Ben Yehuda Street, a Jerusalem boulevard. A sense of the terrible immediacy of the outside world impinges on me, yet there is also something unreal about the sight of bloodstained, immobile bodies being put in to ambulances. I know I am in the presence of a major human event even as the thought that I would have had a coffee in this street in the next day or two passes through my mind. Slowly a feeling of anger wells up – why does this have to happen? It has been expected for some time. Now the recriminations will begin. Netanyahu pouring scorn on the peace process and blaming the Palestinians for failing to keep in check the militancy his policies are helping to foment. Hamas acting with violence and rejecting the negotiating table. This is the second bombing in a few months. The extremists on both sides play in to each other's hands. I realise some kind of change has occurred in the atmosphere in Daoud's living room – bitterness, disillusion, a feeling of having experienced all this before? Daoud says a 'closure' will come.

The next day the details became clear. Six were killed and 137 injured. Hamas has claimed responsibility. A 'closure' has been imposed – Israeli soldiers have put the Palestinians under siege. People are wearily used to this tactic, a collective punishment for the bombing. Although it may help in the search for the killers, it must surely be more an expression of anger and despair or a futile attempt to get the population to reject militant fundamentalism than an effective security measure. It has a bludgeoning effect on the whole community and it seems to strengthen support for Hamas rather than the opposite. Soldiers are now preventing Palestinians moving outside their town or village; the country will come virtually to a standstill and no one will be allowed into Israel for work. As a foreigner I can travel, if I can find the means, but Palestinian students, businessmen, pregnant mothers, the ill and the aged and anyone else with an urgent reason to move may not. By the middle of the month the closure has pushed unemployment in Balata camp beyond 80%. Because it is thought that schools will suffer most in forthcoming cuts in the UNRWA budget, the refugees, surely again more in despair than hope, have organised a strike against UNRWA, their chief if ailing benefactor.

Khalil is at his wits' ends. He said on the phone today, 'I will be heavily fined if Israeli troops catch me trying to get to the university by using the minor roads to by-pass the road blocks. This is too undignified for me to cope with.' In a voice cracking with emotion he went on, 'I am in effect a refugee now. I have no passport or citizenship and no one represents me to the outside world. Look at the daily realities. Israel is constantly appropriating Arab land without real censure from the international community. And serious social decay cannot be put off much longer. Schoolteachers are so badly paid now that many work after hours in Israel in order to get by.' I listened in bafflement and could find no words to soften his pain.

The closure impinges on my own world. As the days pass I realise I am closer to the sharp edge of political events than 18 months ago. The closure back in October 1995 was winding down just as I arrived. I'm now experiencing the sheer banality and boredom of restricted choice. Most refugees go through this kind of thing every day. This has thrown me onto my own resources. In Khalil's absence our interviewing trips are off. He usually arranges them a day or two ahead to ensure that people are available. I can fix some meetings myself but Khalil's presence offers the interviewees reassurance. There is now little to fill my time except my own company or socialising. Khalil's absence has depressed my energy and it raises a question mark over the whole project. This is where Ziad could help though.

I took a taxi to Balata. After Ziad and I had caught up on our lives he re-introduces me to a member of the Legislative Council who also heads a large organisation that represents refugees here and in the diaspora, Husam Khader (real name). Husam is well used to dealing with interviews, usually with journalists from the world's media. Although he is developing a considerable political reputation he continues to live in Balata Camp. He is a dynamo of a man – quick-talking, answering his aides and the telephone in a jocular, incisive manner while carrying on a conversation with me. His record and forceful personality command attention. I know of no other Palestinian MP below ministerial rank to whom a British newspaper has devoted an article: *The Guardian* called him 'the quintessential Palestinian hero.' He has a strong sense of history and past injustices; they may have given him his clarity of vision. He is of humble origins – his grandfather was a policeman in Jaffa Railway Station – but his father had a lengthy schooling and passed on to his children his dream of return to his place of birth. 'We want to go back because it was so beautiful and Balata is not,' he explained. He was deported to Lebanon on the orders of Israeli Prime Minister Rabin in 1988 before leading a wandering life with the PLO. He missed most of the intifada. His last memories of the West Bank before going abroad were of the 'glory period' just before the intifada, in 1984-87, when the Palestinians were evolving a new form of society. Fatah had the support of virtually everyone – 'Fatah and the people moved hand in hand' – and Israeli troops were not allowed into the camp. He returned from Tunis in 1994 to a world in disarray – the 'worst days.' Israeli closures were frequent, the Palestinian authorities were forfeiting the people's trust, and families were looking to their own interests. He has crossed swords with Arafat on a number of occasions and is seen as the leader of the unofficial opposition to him. He is appalled by the corruption and autocratic attitudes amongst the Palestinian leadership.

Husam Khader is presently embroiled in a fight with the mayor of Nablus, Ghassan Shaka'a (real name). This seems to be a good, old-fashioned fight between two Fatah grandees to see who holds political sway in the Nablus area in the vacuum left by the Israeli withdrawal. The tussle also plays upon old 'town versus refugee camp' antipathies. Refugees did well in the 1996 election to the Legislative Council. Three Balata candidates, including Khader, were elected out of the seven for the Nablus area. Shaka'a's name carries as much weight in Nablus as does Khader's in the camps. The mayor is an attorney involved in local business; he is under Arafat's wing and he sits on the executive of the PLO. He became popular in the town when he set about cleaning it up two years ago. Khader's most recent populist action is to get people in two local camps to refuse to pay the increase in water bills that followed the introduction of water meters on the orders of Mayor Shaka'a. The town authorities responded firstly by cutting off the camps' water supply and, a little later, by Shaka'a and the council resigning. Arafat appointed a committee to sort the dispute out but its members include two men whose impartiality Shaka'a has questioned. One was born in Balata and the other is in any case a sworn enemy of Shaka'a. A stand-off continues. A local journalist is reported to have told the *Palestine Report* newspaper: 'The people have discovered that they are not good men, that they are mostly concerned with themselves and getting [power] for themselves.'

I am beginning to feel less tuned in to the daily political situation now, partly because of the effect of the closure on the interview programme and partly because I have joined up with a group of well-established friends – Palestinian, English, French and Belgian. On one occasion we visited an Arab restaurant a few miles away in the joint Palestinian-Israeli patrolled area. The setting was beautiful, the situation infinitely sad. We sat in a large courtyard high on a ridge looking down to the lights of scattered villages. We could see to eat by the light of the large, bright stars. Yet only one other table was in use beside our own. There were as many waiters as customers. The food was excellent. The setting was theatrical. Yet, the incongruity of such tasteful service in an area made inaccessible for many people because of the military patrols, a situation in which we foreigners are very fortunate, weighed heavily on me and I was glad we didn't stay long. When I mentioned my reservations to a European friend he replied, 'Yes, it is dangerous to stay in the West Bank too long. We might easily take our privileged position for granted.' The restaurant is just the kind of enterprise the Palestine National Authority want to encourage. One of our party said it was the brainchild of a returnee. Its future looks bleak. It is not possible to avoid politics in this land. It infiltrates everywhere.

With time to spare I try to make sense of the impressions I've gained from my friends' scattered comments on Palestinian society and its relations with Israel. A difference emerges between the testimony of Ziad and Hassan (and Husam) on the one hand and Khalil, Walid and Mahmoud on the other. The first three men are camp dwellers, the families of the second group have uncontested possession of resources, landed or business. This difference seems to have coloured their opinions. Anger and a sense of deprivation give a distinct tone to the words of Ziad and his friends. Their lives are held in suspension by loss. The property-owning men are able to keep their lives moving forward. They are not overloaded with resentment and unresolved feelings; they have hope and can for the most part live in the present. This is not to say that they are free of rancour. Suffering the indignity of the 'closure' in September 1997, Khalil identified with the refugees. After the Israelis killed Yahyah Ayyash the Hamas bomb maker in mid-November 1995 Walid talked gloomily of Arabs and Jews never living side by side. Mahmoud was so depressed at the prospect of another intifada that he planned to move to America for the children of his future marriage. All three men knew they could go abroad and the Israelis would let them return. In contrast, most camp men have a security record because they were at the forefront of fighting in the intifada. They cannot travel abroad or work in Israel. They are trapped by history and circumstances. It is tempting to see camp refugees as the reactionary and warrior-like obstacles to movement on the Palestinian side of the peace negotiations. This is the opposite of the case here, however. For sure, Ziad and Hassan refer frequently to their grandfathers who owned land in present-day Israel; moreover, these young men have lived their entire lives in the camp. Their bitterness is manifest in words and deeds. They (and Husam Khader) are political activists and yet they are all loyal to the mainstream (and in terms of the peace process, moderate) Fatah party. I wonder if this has something to do with the pride all three men show in the lives of their forebears in their pre-1948 villages and towns? All have seen action against Israeli troops or armed settlers and yet they are dedicated to a party led by autocratic Arafat, who is probably as near as it is possible to get today to a certain type of old-style clan leader. All were assiduous university students. There is no revolutionary spark here – whether against Israel or the Palestinian leadership. Husam Khader criticises Arafat and 'the mafia' that, he says, runs the Palestinian Authority, but he stays loyal to Fatah, Arafat's party. Zaid and Hassan are happy with the moderate changes envisaged by the PLO leadership of Arafat's generation. I remember Ziad proudly pointing to two photographs on the Fatah office wall, both of him standing with Arafat, one on a tour of the West Bank by some Balata residents, the other with a football team playing in Jordan. It is surely to men like this that the West and Israel should be appealing. Solid, caring, responsible and open to gradual changes in a direction the West can understand, while respecting what traditional society holds dear. And these are camp dwellers, men who were feared by Israeli soldiers during the intifada! Would that Israeli politicians, who tend to see Palestinians and especially refugees as firebrands, could observe Ziad today on his way to work in Ramallah – the civil servant, briefcase in hand.

Israeli troops have raided some nearby villages, included Assyra al-Shamaliya, where I spent pleasant hours taking tea with two families in 1995. Over 500 young men have been arrested. Assyra is in the area jointly controlled (under the peace accords) by Israeli and Palestinian troops, just outside Palestinian territory. The entire Nablus area has been declared 'a closed military zone.' This is a follow-up to the recent bombings in Jerusalem's Mahane (Market) Yehuda and Ben Yehuda Street. Five young men from Assyra, who are missing, are thought to belong to a Hamas military unit; four of them are being linked to suicide bombers responsible for the Jerusalem bombings. Unrest is high on the Palestinian side over US approval for extremist Israeli settlers to stay in houses they have occupied in the Ras al-Amoud district of Arab East Jerusalem. Here in Nablus things have slowed down; my local vegetable market is sparsely provisioned and attended. Hassan said there is talk in the camps of another intifada – 'life is a prison here.' I can see why – unemployment, closures, the Israeli and the Palestinian leaders swapping epithet and rancour – things look as black as they can be, a non-peace process by any other name.

The Palestinians have their internal problems of course. I saw little at first hand to indicate a popular response to the presence of a new elite, the PLO returnees from exile in Tunis, except for one small but telling incident. Going with Walid to visit his fiancée in Refidia one day we noticed that a small window had been smashed in a large new Mercedes saloon car parked nearby. Walid reported this to the owner, a senior police officer, recently returned from Tunis. This gentleman was angry and sent his armed lieutenant cum bodyguard out to inspect the damage. Is this the tip of an iceberg? How many other small resentments are being expressed in extra-parliamentary and illegal ways throughout the town? Except in the rhetoric of Husam Khader there might be no other outlet for these feelings.

As departure drew near again I began to speculative about the future. The land here is so small; tough decisions will have to be made if both peoples are to inhabit it under a just settlement. Yet there is little public sign of creative thinking that will break the mould as yet. Things have stood still or regressed in 18 months. Negotiations run into the same walls, built to protect old pain and anguish. Perhaps the intifada and Rabin's response to it were the only occasions when it could truly be said that people in this land took control of their own destinies by rejecting the predictable. The threatening, cataclysmic language of leaders when an impasse occurs is one of the most predictable of outcomes. It only states the obvious to say that the ability to rise above the storm and look to a benevolent, longer-term outcome is the region's only hope. In addition, in this land of old, remembered pain, it will very likely require the making of some generous acts of redemption and atonement.

The problem seems insoluble. It is, in the words of an Israeli columnist, 'unsettling to live with the complex insight that the conflict here in the holy land is between two just causes and between two true narratives that contradict each other.'[1] Perhaps there are as yet too many absolutes to cope with – as represented by the word 'contradict' for example – which serve to entrench the opposites ever more deeply. A larger truth still eludes us. Yet, hard as it is, we must keep looking for that truth or remain in thrall to fear, pride and old assumptions. The peace negotiators must keep hearing the same laments and demands from the opposing side. Do they sometimes catch themselves wondering if this is an echo, before they again reach a wall constructed from old injustices, and retreat, perhaps to try again? Can they bear their own pain without being overwhelmed, believe they are being heard, and trust that the other side is struggling like this too? This is a new territory, a creatively sought after and perhaps blessed ground.

---

(1) Ruvik Rosenthal, in *The Jerusalem Report*, 11 October 1999.

CHAPTER 12

Newcastle

LETTERS JAM MY post box. The flat is quiet, waiting. It is cool after the outside temperature, which unusually is little short of Nablus's. The sun etches arabesques from the window curtain onto the opposite wall. Random memories of the last few weeks chase through my mind. Familiar faces are not far away. But my mind drifts away and I lose a sense of time. For a moment I am part of a universe that does not distinguish between this spot and 'out there'. After a while the sensation fades and I pick up the phone.

Bibliography

There is an exhaustive literature on all aspects of the Israeli-Palestinian conflict. Books that have particularly helped me are:

Said K Aburish, *Children of Bethany: the Story of a Palestinian Family* (London, Bloomsbury, 1991 edition)

A Survey of Palestine (*Prepared in December 1945 and January 1946 for the Information of the Anglo-American Committee of Inquiry*), 2 volumes and supplement, (Washington, Institute for Palestine Studies, 1991 printing).

Norman and Helen Bentwich, *Mandate Memories 1918-1948* (London, Hogarth, 1965)

Beshara Doumani, *Rediscovering Palestine: Merchants and Peasants in Jabal Nablus 1700-1900* (London, University of California Press, 1995).

Thomas Friedman, *From Beirut to Jerusalem; One Man's Middle East Odyssey* (London, William Collins, 1990)

Emile Habiby, *The Secret Life of Saeed, the Ill-Fated Pessoptimist* (Columbia LA, USA, Readers International, 1974;1989)

David Horovitz, *Yitzhak Rabin: Soldier of Peace* (London, Peter Halban, 1996)

Eunice Holliday, *Letters from Jerusalem during the Palestine Mandate* (ed. John C Holliday) (London, Radcliffe Press, 1997)

Anton Jirku, *The World of the Bible* (London, Weidenfeld and Nicolson, 1957)

David Pryce-Jones, *The Face of Defeat: Palestinian Refugees and Guerrillas* (London, Quartet, 1974)

Walid Khalili (ed) *All That Remains: The Palestinian Villages Occupied and Destroyed by Israel in 1948* (Washington, Institute for Palestine Studies, 1992)

Arthur Koestler, *Promise and Fulfilment: Palestine 1917-1949* (London, MacMillan, 1949)

Walter Laqueur, *A History of Zionism* (London, Weidenfeld and Nicolson, 1972)

Dominic Lieven, 'Dilemmas of Empire, 1850-1918. Power, Territory, Identity.' *Journal of Contemporary History*, 34 (2) (1999) pp 67-196

David McDowall, *The Palestinians* (London, The Minority Rights Group, Report No. 24, 1987)

Fergus Millar, *The Roman Near East, 31 BC-AD 337* (Cambridge, Mass. and London, Harvard University Press, 1993)

Mary E Mills, *Historical Israel: Biblical Israel; Studying Joshua to 2 Kings* (London, Cassell, 1999)

Benny Morris, *The Birth of the Palestinian Refugee Problem, 1947-49* (Cambridge, Cambridge University Press, 1987).

Edward W Said, *The Question of Palestine* (London, Vintage, 1992)

Ze'ev Schiff and Ehud Ya'ari, *Intifada. The Palestinian Uprising – Israel's Third Front* (New York, Touchstone, 1991)

Kirsten E Schulze, *The Israeli-Arab Conflict* (London, Longman, 1999)

Salman Abu-Sitta, *Palestine 1948. 50 Years after Nakba* (London, Palestine Return Centre, 1998)

Graham Usher, *Dispatches from Palestine: The Rise and Fall of the Oslo Peace Process* (London, Pluto Press, 1999)

Index

Abdul, 52, 53
Abraham, 8, 31
Abu Fathi, 12, 21
Abu Mustafa, 12
Aburish, Said K, 53, 54
Abu Tarik, 12, 15, 18
Afif, 86, 88
Ahmad, 72, 74
Ali, Muhammad, 28
Al-Kafrein, 9, 10, 21
Al-Karemeh, battle of, 18
Amman, 45, 75
Al-Nakba, 9
Al-Sawalma, 68,72
Al-Umar, Zahir, 26
An Najah University, 26, 34, 35, 45, 50, 51, 72, 88, 101
Arab Al-Sawalma, 68, 72
Arabia, Saudi, 23
Arabic, 64
Arabs, 2, 3, 4, 5, 6, 10, 14, 20, 21, 24, 25, 37, 39, 40, 49, 89, 100, 103, 104
   Discontent, 30
   Customs and society, 38, 51, 52, 53, 54, 55, 56, 59, 64-65, 73, 81, 82, 90
Arafat, Yassir, vii, 19, 23, 30, 45, 57, 69, 70, 79-80, 84, 85, 88, 90, 95, 103, 105
Assyra al-Shamaliya, 51, 105-106
Assyrians, 48
Ayya, 40
Ayyash, Yahya, 84, 85, 100, 104

Baathist, 14
Balfour Declaration, 3, 69, 70
   Day, 70

Barak, Ehud, 46
Bedouin, 35f, 59, 68, 69, 73, 81
Beirut, 13, 18, 28
Beit Sahour peace group, 61, 62, 63, 84
Begin, Menachem, 47
Belsen camp, viii
Ben Gurion, David, 9, 46
Benny, 52
Bethany, 53
Bethlehem, 56-57, 63
   University, 57
   Church of the Nativity, 57
Bilad Es-Shaam, 82

Cairo, 28
Cars, stolen, 90
Chalcolithic town, 31
Christians, 88
   Eastern Orthodox, 32-33
Communists, 14, 20, 22
Crossman, Richard, 33
Crusaders, 31, 33

Damascus, 28
Daoud, 35, 54
David, 48
Dayan, General, 46
Democratic Front, 20
Dir Yassin, 6

Earthquake, 1927, 29, 32, 36
   1995, 75
Ebal, Mt, 30, 34, 44, 51, 81
Egypt/Egyptians, vii, 16, 55, 56, 75, 80, 94
Ein Kerem, 63
Erez checkpoint, 89

111

European Election Observers, 41, 50, 95

Fatah, 20, 21, 22, 68, 70, 73, 78, 85, 88, 95, 103, 105
  Hawks, 42

Gaddafy, Colonel, 23
Galilee, 6
Gaza Strip and City, 6, 18, 23, 24, 41, 47, 56, 65, 72, 83, 84, 89-96
  Housing, 94-95, 96, 97
Gerizim, Mt 26, 30, 31, 32, 35, 48, 49
Germany, 78
Golan Heights, 47
Gordimer, Nadine, 97
Green Line, 4, 16, 63
Guardian, The, 102
Gulf War, 23, 47

Haifa, 6, 9
Hamas, 20, 21, 22, 41, 69, 78, 85, 100, 101, 104, 105, 106
Hanan, 92
Hanukkah, 63
Hassan, 69, 70, 71, 75, 77, 84, 93, 99, 104, 105, 106
Hebrew, 61, 89
Hebron/Hebronites, 23, 55
Hizbulla, 47, 87, 100
Holon (Israel), 49
Hussein, Saddam, 23

Ibrahim, 72, 73, 89-95
lnstanbul, American University of, 36
Iraq, 16, 23
Islam, 39, 49, 54, 64, 84, 88
  Islamic Jihad, 40
  Islamic Orthodox, 18, 21, 37, 38, 40, 83
Israel, 4, 6, 7, 14, 16, 17, 18, 19, 21, 24, 36, 40, 41, 45, 54, 57, 61, 68, 69, 70, 71, 72, 74, 77, 79, 85, 100, 101-102, 104, 105
Israeli
  Closure, 23, 71, 83, 101-102, 103, 104
  Election, 57, 87
  Occupation, vii, 7, 16, 17, 22, 30, 34, 37, 41, 45, 51, 52, 53, 54, 57, 62, 66, 68, 70, 82, 83, 85, 86-87, 88, 90, 93, 97, 101-102
  Security Services, 7, 19, 33, 36, 41, 42, 44, 46, 59-60, 61-62, 66, 69, 78, 81, 82, 86, 89, 97, 100, 103, 105
  Settlements/settlers, 15, 24, 32, 58, 59-60, 78, 100, 105
  Village Leagues, 54

Jaba', 56
Jacob, 31
Jacob's Well, 32-33
Jaffa, 6, 45, 69, 102
Jenin, 9, 15
Jericho, 11, 23, 36
Jerusalem, 3, 4, 5, 6, 7, 9, 22, 23, 28, 30, 31, 32, 48, 51, 53, 57, 58, 59, 60, 61, 63, 86, 89, 96
  Al-Aqsa Mosque, 68, 97
  Ben Yehuda Street, 61, 63, 100-101, 105
  Damascus Gate, 60
  Haram Al-Sharif, 69
  Mahane Yehuda, 105
  Muslim Quarter, 62
  Old City, 24, 60-62, 96
  Ras Al-Moud district, 106
Jerusalem Times, The, 74
Jesus, 31-32, 57
Jewish Agency, 9
  Aliya, 3, 7
  Christian persecution of, viii
  Holocaust, viii, 4
  National Home, 3, 4, 6, 7
  Defence forces, 5, 6, 9, 10
  Orthodox, 3
  Pogroms, 2
  Refugees, 4, 7, 33
  Russian immigrants, 7, 69
  Zionists, 2, 6, 10, 11, 33, 87
Jews, 3, 5, 6, 71, 82-83, 84, 104
John, 41, 43, 87
John's Gospel, 32
John the Baptist, 31
Jokes, regional, 55-56

112

Jordan/Jordanians, 1, 6, 7, 14, 15, 16, 17, 36, 43, 55-56, 70, 83, 105
Joseph, 31
Joseph's Tomb, 24, 31, 32, 97
Joshua, 48
Judaism, 49, 63
Judea, 48
Juha, 56
Justinian, Emperor, 49

Khader, Husam, 76, 102-103, 104, 105
Khalil, 26, 34-35, 36, 40, 41, 45, 51, 52-57, 64, 72, 82, 97, 99, 101, 104
Khalil, Sameeha, 95
Koran, 44, 64, 84
Kuwait, 23

Labour/One Nation Party, 46, 86
Latrun, 5, 6, 9
Lawrence, T E, ix
League of Nations, 3
Lebanon, 7, 46, 47, 65, 86, 100, 102
  'Grapes of Wrath' assault on, 96, 100
Libya, 23
Likud Party, 86
Lud, 69
Lydda, 46

Maher, 45
Mahmoud, 43, 45-46, 47, 51, 76, 82, 93, 99, 104
Massih, Abdel, 22
Mecca, 64, 83
Meretz Party, 86
Mesopotamia, 49
Mishmar ha-Emeq, 9
Mona, 89-90, 95
Mohammed, 64
Morton, H V, 38
Moses, 48, 49
Mousa, 88
Muslims, 16, 21, 33, 37, 41, 81, 84, 100

Nablus/Neapolis, 1, 4, 5, 8, 13, 14, 15, 23, 24, 25-44, 46, 48, 49, 50, 51, 58, 60, 61, 67, 68, 71, 74, 75, 76, 77, 78, 79, 81, 82, 83, 84, 86, 93, 94, 99, 100, 103, 105, 106, 108
  Al-Hussein Square, 26, 35, 41
  Big Families of, 28-29, 30
  Municipality/al-baladiyya, 68, 84
  Old City, 26, 29-30, 35, 49, 50, 100
  Rafidia district, 35, 49-50, 106
  Romans in, 31, 34
  Samaritans in, 31, 32, 33, 47, 49, 88
Nazareth, 46
Negev Desert, 6
Netanyahu, Benyamin, 47, 56, 78, 96, 97, 100, 101
Newcastle upon Tyne, 1, 97, 108

Oslo Peace Process, 23, 43, 46, 47, 57, 70, 75, 76-77, 79, 85, 86, 87, 92, 95, 100, 101, 106
Ottoman Empire, 2, 26, 28, 29, 36

Palestine, 1, 5, 6, 8, 10, 13, 49, 54, 68
  British Mandate in, 1, 4, 5, 26, 33, 36, 40, 51, 53, 82
Palestine Liberation Organisation (PLO), 14, 15, 16, 17, 18, 23, 41, 47, 68, 69, 82, 87, 94, 95, 102, 103, 105, 106
Palestine Report, The, 103
Palestinian Collaborators, 53-54, 75, 93-94
  Customs, 46, 88
  Election, 50-51, 87-88, 94-96
  Fedayeen, 14
  Intifada, 17, 18, 19, 30, 36, 41, 42, 44, 47, 53, 66, 68-69, 74, 76, 80, 83, 87, 102. 103, 104, 106
  Police, 36, 43, 86, 89, 90, 99, 105
  Research Centre, 50
  Universities, ix, 74, 88
Palestinian National Authority (PNA), 42, 53, 72, 74, 79, 83, 85, 90, 92, 96, 99, 105
  Legislative Assembly, 96, 102, 103

Partridge's Dictionary, 40
Pathe News, viii
Peace Now, 86
Peres, Shimon, 78, 87, 96, 100
Persian language, 64
Philistines, 33
Pontius Pilate, 49
Popular Front, 20

Qana, 100
Quakers, 63-64

Rabin, Yitzhak, 19, 23, 46, 47, 57, 78, 85, 96, 100, 102, 106
Ramadan, 95
Ramallah, 4, 12, 24, 25, 38, 56, 58-59, 60, 63, 99, 105
Ramleh, 46
Rashedah, 72-74
Refugees, ix, 1, 6, 7, 8-24, 30-31, 33, 45-46, 53, 59, 66-80, 87, 88, 89-90, 92-93, 101,102, 103, 104, 105
  Committee for the Defence of Palestinian Refugee Rights, 76
  Camps: Asker, 76
    Balata, 14, 31, 33, 66-78, 93, 97, 99, 101, 102, 103, 105
    Beach, 94
    Fari'a, 8-22, 42, 66, 67, 68, 72, 78-80
    Jabalia, 73
    Education in, 71-75
    Employment in, 71, 101
Return Review, The, 78-79
Rishou, 26, 39
Rose, 40
Roumania, 2
Russia, 7,
Ruth, 86-87, 96

Saladin, 31-32
Samaria, 48, 49
Sanai, 48

Saudi Arabia, 23
Sawalima, 21
Shaka'a, Ghassan, 103
Shamir, Yitzhak, 47
Sharon, General, 46, 47
Sheikh, 35
Shekhem, 8, 31, 3 3
Solomon, 48
Syria/Syrians, 7, 16, 47, 55-56, 75, 82

Tel Aviv, 1, 2, 5, 46
Tubas, 8
Tulkarm, 39
Tunis, 19, 88, 90, 106

Uganda, 2
Um Al-Zianat, 21
United Nations, 4, 5, 6, 8, 12, 24, 70
United Nations Relief and Works Agency (UNRWA), 12, 14, 15, 20, 68, 72, 74-75, 79, 93, 101

Vespasian, Emperor, 49

Walaa, Sheikh, 18, 21
Walid, 45, 81-84, 88, 104
War, 1914-18, 2, 3, 40
  1939-45, 4, 40
  1948, 4, 5, 9, 10, 14, 46, 73, 79, 93
  1967, 6, 15, 16, 46, 76, 78, 93
West Bank, 1, 4, 6, 7, 8, 14, 16, 18, 23, 24, 30, 36, 37, 38, 41, 44, 45, 46, 47, 50, 51, 55, 56, 62, 65, 67, 81, 82, 83, 93, 96, 97, 98, 102, 104, 105
Woman at the Well, 32, 49

Yassin, Sheikh, 41

Zakkaria, 69, 93
Ziad, 66, 69-73, 75, 77, 78, 82, 99, 102, 104, 105